Several Factors Have Historically Extended the Lifespan of a Civilization

These Factors Are Weak, or Missing, in the United States Today

C. E. Nough

Table of Contents

CHAPTER 1: INTRODUCTION

A civilization, as opposed to packs of animals, can be described by:

- ➢ A sufficient and secure food supply
- ➢ Cities as an organizing structure
- ➢ Labor specialization
- ➢ Social and economic organizations
- ➢ An organized and stable government
- ➢ Writing.

Most of these factors are eroding in the United States.

Instead of creating and guarding community strengths and values, individualist animalistic behaviors are increasingly emerging.

Factors that have historically contributed to a civilization's survival (and were present in the early history of the United States) are gone due to mismanagement by leadership and globalization:

- ➢ Natural protective boundaries
- ➢ Reliable and stable food supply
- ➢ Small reliance on external resources
- ➢ Revered, prime leadership (historically kings and the divine).

Again, these saving features are gone in the United States.

The purpose of this book is to study the animal heritage of humans, and the development and fall of historical civilizations, and to suggest just how shaky the foundations of the United States may now be.

A harbinger of the current state can be found in the 2016 Presidential competition. There are two camps of political thought:

1. The United States is still the greatest power on Earth, which may need a few tweaks
2. The United States is seriously flawed, and needs to change direction.

A clue is that the populace in 2016 has proposed candidates and supported them electorally that would NEVER have been considered in the past 100 years.

The common goal of the United States? Community Interests versus Individual Interests?

1. Humans are animals (though many would like to selectively forget that), so we will explore our animal heritage.

When I was in graduate school in Psychology, one of the most revealing courses I took was "Comparative Animal Psychology" – what traits are found in the animal kingdom that we humans have as our heritage, and possibly some innate tendencies to still mimic. From the basic needs of the single celled animal, to our close neighbors on the evolutionary tree: the mammals.

This course was not part of a Psychology core curriculum, but offered because we happened to be lucky enough to have an expert on the Faculty.

Bottom line: we inherit and display a lot of behavior traits with our fellow animals.

2. Civilizations Have Been Formed to Best Satisfy Survival and Smooth Interpersonal Interactions. But Do They?

In "Civilization" class, my professor made reference to the most highly civilized nation that ever lived, the Persian Empire. His claim was that, "A naked, virgin woman with a bag of gold could walk from one edge of the empire to the farthest edge, and lose nothing!"

As my life unfolded, I came to see individual human and societal "problems" mostly as the juggling between animal instincts and with the requirements of a well-functioning society.

Many World philosophies and religions have a root core of statements about the need for humans to control animal instincts for the greater good of the community.

CHAPTER 2: THE ANIMAL HERITAGE

I am going to quote extensively from experts (and better writers) with a series of ideas. My contribution is providing the guiding thread through them.

Characteristics of our animal ancestors:

Animals Lie to Each Other

For example,

> When in a tight spot, animals 'lie' to their own kind to get what they want, a University of Rochester biologist has found.
>
> By proving that the weaker are able to deceive the stronger to survive, Adams' findings runs counter to a common belief by biologists that communication within a species must always be reliable and honest.[1]

And

> Take for example Koko the Gorilla[2]. When her handlers confronted her after she tore a steel sink out of its mooring, she signed "cat did it" and pointed at her innocent pet kitten....
>
> The better a creature is at lying, bluffing, and deceiving, the more likely it is to survive in this world. Lying is all about deceiving predators and surviving - whether it is an insect changing its colors, or a human lying to a boss who might fire him

---

[1] Do Animals "Lie"? Yes, Even to Their Own Kind, Biologist Says. Retrieved from: http://www.rochester.edu/news/show.php?id=1421

[2] Koko is a Gorilla who has learned many hand signs from a modified version of American Sign Language.

and take away his income and means of survival. [3]

Areas where animals lie:

Desirable-mate Issues

Deceptive alarm calls are used by male swallows (*Hirundo rustica*). Males give these false alarm calls when females leave the nest area during the mating season, and are thus able to disrupt extra-pair copulations. As this is likely to be costly to females, it can be seen as an example of sexual conflict.[4]

Resources, Such As Food

Counterfeit alarm calls are also used by thrushes to avoid intraspecific competition. By sounding a bogus alarm call normally used to warn of aerial predators, they can frighten other birds away, allowing them to eat undisturbed.[5]

Desirable Territory

When resources are plentiful, and an animal finds a food cache, they usually call their own and share.

When resources are scarce, animals may quickly abandon a resource, act natural, and return later alone.

---

[3] http://www.healthdiaries.com/animals-lie.htm
[4] Retrieved from: https://en.wikipedia.org/wiki/Alarm_signal#False_alarm_calls
[5] Ibid.

Animals Steal

Oh, these cunning creatures. In behavior that requires athleticism and grace as well as planning and decision making, kleptoparasitic animals prove that it really is a dog-eat-dog world out there. Using this sly foraging strategy, animal thieves steal food already procured by other animals. If you've ever had a brazen seagull snatch a sandwich from your picnic at the beach, you've played host to a kleptoparasite. And gulls aren't the only guileful ones — the following are some of the animals especially adept at pulling a fast one when it comes to pilfering a meal.

Eagles, Western Gulls, Chinstrap Penguins, Sperm Whales, Hyenas, Dew Drop Spiders, Water Crickets, and Cuckoo Bees.[6]

Species Coexistence

The term **niche differentiation** (synonymous with niche segregation, niche separation and niche partitioning), as it applies to the field of ecology, refers to the process by which competing species use the environment differently in a way that helps them to coexist. The competitive exclusion principle states that if two species with identical niches (i.e., ecological roles) compete, then one will inevitably drive the other to extinction. When two species differentiate their niches, they tend to compete less strongly, and are thus more likely to coexist. Species can differentiate their niches in many ways, such as by consuming different foods, or using different parts of the environment. -- Wikipedia

---

[6] *Kleptoparasites: 8 animals that steal from others*
Retrieved from: http://www.mnn.com/earth-matters/animals/photos/kleptoparasites-8-animals-steal-food-others/related-photos

Inter-Species Competition for Resources

Biologists typically recognize two types of competition: interference and exploitative competition. During interference competition, organisms interact directly by fighting for scarce resources. For example, large aphids defend feeding sites on cottonwood leaves by kicking and shoving smaller aphids from better sites. In contrast, during exploitative competition, organisms interact indirectly by consuming scarce resources.

For example, plants consume nitrogen by absorbing it into their roots, making nitrogen unavailable to nearby plants. Plants that produce many roots typically reduce soil nitrogen to very low levels, eventually killing neighboring plants.

Male-male competition in red deer during rut is an example of interference competition within a species.

-Interference Competition-

Occurs *directly* between individuals via aggression etc. when the individuals interfere with foraging, survival, reproduction of others, or by directly preventing their physical establishment in a portion of the habitat. An example of this can be seen between the ant *Novomessor cockerelli* and red harvester ants, where the former interferes with the ability of the latter to forage by plugging the entrances to their colonies with small rocks.

-Exploitation Competition-

Occurs *indirectly* through a common limiting resource which acts as an intermediate. For example, use of resources depletes the amount available to others, or they compete for space. Also known as exploitative competition.

-Apparent Competition-

Occurs *indirectly* between two species which are both preyed upon by the same predator. For example, species A and species B are both prey of predator C. The increase of species A may cause the decrease of species B, because the increase of A's may aid in the survival of predator C's, which will increase the number of predator C's, which in turn will hunt more of species B. -- Wikipedia

Animals Kill Their Own

Animals unquestionably kill members of their species, all the time. Male lions slaughter all the cubs when they join a new pride; rival ant colonies of the same species fight bloody wars; chimpanzees have been shown to kill each other at similar per capita rates to humans."[7]

Ants are the only species besides humans that carry out wars and enslave their own. And by enslave we mean pulling out the ant whips and putting the other guy to work against his will.

When they're not doing that, they like to tear each other limb from limb.[8]

And

Bottle nose dolphins besides also being among the smartest things on Earth, share another characteristic with humans: they're the only other animal that will kill for fun.

[7] Retrieved from: http://www.sciencefocus.com/qa/do-animals-murder-their-own-species
[8] Retrieved from: http://www.cracked.com/article_16762_the-6-biggest-assholes-in-animal-kingdom.html

Back in the late nineties, marine biologists began to find lots of porpoise carcasses that had seemingly been punched in the gut until they died. After rounding up the suspects, putting them in the line up, the porpoise widow pointed at the guilty party: ... bottle-nose dolphins.[9]

Animal Sexual Fidelity

The evolution of mating systems in animals has received an enormous amount of attention from biologists. This section briefly reviews three main findings about the evolution of monogamy in animals.

The amount of social monogamy in animals varies across taxa, with over 90% of birds engaging in social monogamy while only 3% of mammals are known to do the same.[10]

Three Animal Responses to Habitat Change

When the habitat/environment changes, such as with food supply or climate, animals have three responses to the change:

- Adapt genetically
- Internally shut down reproduction
- Search out and move to a new habitat
- Reduce numbers via killing within species.

Adapt

In 2005, a group of scientists from La Trobe University in Australia investigated how species will adapt to global warming by studying a species of rainforest fly, *Drosophila birchii* (later published in *Science*). Increased temperatures may lead to drier conditions in rainforests, so the authors wanted to

---

[9] ibid
[10] Retrieved from: https://en.wikipedia.org/wiki/Monogamy_in_animals#Monogamous_species

see how quickly this fly could adapt and develop resistance to desiccation.

As in many directed evolution experiments, they took the flies to a lab and exposed them to dry conditions, with most of the flies unable to survive the dryness. The survivors were then bred to one another. Thus generation after generation, only the most desiccation resistant flies would survive, resulting in a population that could survive dry conditions potentially induced by global warming. Right?

Well, that was the idea at least. At first, their population of flies did show a bit of increased resistance. However, in the proceeding 28 generations of selection, there was no increased resistance to desiccation, despite that previous papers had found increased resistance in 3 other *Drosophila* species. *Drosophila birchii* was unable to adapt to these conditions.

What went wrong? ….

Natural selection itself is based on three assumptions in a population. The **first** is that there will be variation in traits, such as multiple colors of eyes or hair. The **second** is that these traits be heritable through the generations, that children will inherit the traits of their parents. The **third** is that these variable traits have differential fitness, or that some versions of a trait might help you survive better than another. Thus certain trait variants will help its carrier organism survive better, passing that trait to its offspring which will in turn bear this trait.

In order for populations to adapt by natural selection, these three requirements must be fulfilled. When a biologist sees any population, he or she typically assumes that these they are met, and I can't really blame them. All cellular life we know of on this planet has a hereditary mechanism, the gene, which has differential fitness depending on the variation, thus meeting requirements two and three….

In Prescot, Merseyside, a copper refinery opened up next to a meadow that had many species of grasses and wildflowers. Over time, the soil was contaminated by copper, killing off many of the plants. However, after 70 years, there were 5 species that were still able to thrive in these meadows! They had adapted and developed a resistance to copper.

Even now I'm thinking to myself, "oh! cool! How did they adapt that way? How did that mechanism work? How quickly did the resistance gene spread?" But what I'm forgetting is that, while five species did adapt, twenty-one species failed to adapt. If there really was massive diversity at all genes in each population, you would think that at least one would confer some benefit to survive the copper. But this did not happen: twenty-one species went locally extinct.

Just as interesting a question as "How did these 5 adapt?" is "Why did these 21 fail to adapt?" But it's a question that's only begun to be reconsidered. *Death and extinction are far more powerful forces in shaping the whole of biodiversity on our planet than successful adaptation* [emphasis mine], but these evolutionary failures that occur all around us are little studied.[11]

Change Individual and Community Behaviors

In the early 1960s, the National Institute of Mental Health (NIMH) acquired property in a rural area outside Poolesville, Maryland. The facility that was built on this property housed several research projects, including those headed by Calhoun. It was here that his most famous experiment, the mouse universe, was created. In July 1968 four pairs of mice were introduced into the Utopian universe. The universe was a 9-foot (2.7 m) square metal pen with 4.5-foot-high (1.4 m) sides. Each side had four groups of four vertical, wire mesh "tunnels." The "tunnels" gave access to nesting boxes, food hoppers, and water

[11] Retrieved from: https://culturingscience.wordpress.com/2011/01/05/when-adaptation-doesnt-happen/

dispensers. There was no shortage of food or water or nesting material. There were no predators. The only adversity was the limit on space....

Initially the population grew rapidly, doubling every 55 days. The population reached 620 by day 315, after which the population growth dropped markedly. The last surviving birth was on day 600. This period between day 315 and day 600 saw a breakdown in social structure and in normal social behavior. Among the aberrations in behavior were the following: expulsion of young before weaning was complete, wounding of young, increase in homosexual behavior, inability of dominant males to maintain the defense of their territory and females, aggressive behavior of females, passivity of non-dominant males with increased attacks on each other which were not defended against. After day 600, the social breakdown continued and the population declined toward extinction. During this period females ceased to reproduce. Their male counterparts withdrew completely, never engaging in courtship or fighting. They ate, drank, slept, and groomed themselves – all solitary pursuits. Sleek, healthy coats and an absence of scars characterized these males. They were dubbed "the beautiful ones." Breeding never resumed and behavior patterns were permanently changed.[12]

Population Migration

Climate change has had a significant direct effect on terrestrial animals, by being a major driver of the processes of speciation and extinction. The best known example of this is the Carboniferous Rainforest Collapse which occurred 350 million years ago. This event decimated amphibian populations and spurred on the evolution of reptiles....

Animals have had specific responses to climate change. Species respond to climate changes by migration, adaptation, or

---

[12] Retrieved from: https://en.wikipedia.org/wiki/John_B._Calhoun#Mouse_experiments

if neither of those occur, death. These migrations can sometimes follow an animal's preferred temperature, elevation, soil, etc., as said terrain moves due to climate change. Adaptation can be either genetic or phenological, and death can occur in a local population only (extirpation) or as an entire species, otherwise known as extinction. – Wikipedia

Alpha Social Structure in Some Animals

In studies of social animals, the highest ranking individual is sometimes designated as the **alpha**. Males, females, or both, can be alphas, depending on the species. Where one male and one female fulfill this role together, they are sometimes referred to as the alpha pair. Other animals in the same social group may exhibit deference or other species-specific subordinate behaviors towards the alpha or alphas.

Alpha animals usually gain preferential access to food and other desirable items or activities, though the extent of this varies widely between species. Male or female alphas may gain preferential access to sex or mates; in some species, only alphas or an alpha pair reproduce.

Alphas may achieve their status by superior physical strength and aggression, or through social efforts and building alliances within the group.

The individual with alpha status sometimes changes, often through a fight between the dominant and a subordinate animal. Such fights may or may not be to the death.[13]

Animal Altruism

You would think it wouldn't pay to be a Meer Kat. These mongoose-like animals from the dry regions of southern Africa

---

[13] https://en.wikipedia.org/wiki/Alpha_%28ethology%29

will postpone meals to help with the baby-sitting. And they will stay home so their family and friends can go out to supper.

Helpful animals? Whatever happened to the evolutionary idea of "survival of the fittest?

And what about the helpful "watchman" bird that lets out a loud squawk when it sees a hawk approaching? All the neighboring flocks know to fly off quickly, which confuses the advancing predator. Yet the alarm-caller puts itself in danger when it calls out. Its give-away squawk may make it a target for attack, while those who heed its alarm get away.

Helpful birds? That seems contrary to "survival of the fittest" too. [14]

Animal Sub-populations

I remember when I was taking my animal-human comparative Psychology course mentioned above, there was a certain fish population that mimicked the Introversion-Extroversion behavior axis in humans.

The behaviorally dominant male population, when resources were plentiful, secured all the healthiest female fish, and the recessive male population died mostly without progeny.

However, when food resources were scarce, the dominant male population went in search of new habitats. Many of these adventurous males died in the process and had no progeny. Meanwhile, back in the original habitat, the recessive males found female mates and kept the home population going.

Nature, by unknown means, kept birthing recessive males to dominant male families.

---

[14] Retrieved from: http://www.creationtips.com/altruists.html

A fight or flight reaction is a response to stress characterized by boosts of adrenaline, dilated pupils and a fast heartbeat. The term was first used in the early 20th century by Walter Cannon, an American physiologist. Cannon used the term to describe animals that underwent situations where they either had to flee or prepare to fight in order to defend themselves from danger. Such a response can also be called *hyperarousal*, or a response to acute stress. According to Cannon's descriptions, when an animal is frightened or imperiled, the sympathetic nervous system responds, causing adrenaline boosts and changes in pupils and heartbeat, and sometimes extra strength shown in bursts of speed if an animal runs away or stays to attack. Some also refer to a third state "fright," occurs when an animal doesn't flee or fight, but panics and passes out or stands still — the typical "deer in the headlights" response or the collapse of sheep if chased by a dog.[15]

---

[15] Retrieved from: http://www.wisegeek.com/what-is-a-fight-or-flight-reaction.htm

CHAPTER 3: CIVILIZATION

Why Do Humans Need Civilization?

Civilization comes from the root "civilized",

- marked by well-organized laws and rules about how people behave with each other
- polite, reasonable, and respectful
- pleasant and comfortable – Merriam Webster Dictionary

Why would humans need to be civilized? (If you skip to the next chapter and look at the lives of hunter-gatherers, it's not so bad!) Answer: when the population grows sufficiently that there are disputes over a limited supply of resources!

Humans love baby-making (though not always baby raising), and <u>so rather than limit population to reduce strife</u>, civilization (socialization) needs to occur.

From the Judeo-Christian standpoint, the commandment to:

> Then God blessed them and said, "Be fruitful and multiply. Fill the earth and govern it. Reign over the fish in the sea, the birds in the sky, and all the animals that scurry along the ground." – Genesis 1:28.

That is probably the only commandment people have obeyed almost universally.

Civilization Defined

> A **civilization** ... is any complex society characterized by urban development, social stratification, symbolic communication forms (typically, writing systems), and a perceived separation from and domination over the natural environment by a cultural elite. Civilizations are intimately associated with and often further defined by other socio-politico-economic characteristics,

including centralization, the domestication of both humans and other organisms, specialization of labor, culturally ingrained ideologies of progress and supremacism, monumental architecture, taxation, societal dependence upon farming as an agricultural practice, and expansionism.

Historically, a *civilization* was a so-called "advanced" culture in contrast to more supposedly primitive cultures. In this broad sense, a civilization contrasts with non-centralized tribal societies, including the cultures of nomadic pastoralists or hunter-gatherers. As an uncountable noun, *civilization* also refers to the process of a society developing into a centralized, urbanized, stratified structure.

Civilizations are organized in densely populated settlements divided into hierarchical social classes with a ruling elite and subordinate urban and rural populations, which engage in intensive agriculture, mining, small-scale manufacture and trade. Civilization concentrates power, extending human control over the rest of nature, including over other human beings. -- Wikipedia

In other words, rather than limit population, humans set up class hierarchies, where (from what resources are available), some inhabitants get all they need (or want), and some inhabitants do without.

The "law" is to prevent rebellion against the system of maldistribution of resources.

Inhabitants are socialized to be "civil" with each other, i.e., polite to the upper class who are screwing them.

Who Is Civilized?

Several person's definitions of "civilized":

> To bring out of a savage, uneducated, or rude state; make civil; elevate in social and private life; enlighten; refine.[16]

> To repress animal nature: "the physical (or animal) side of a person as opposed to the spirit or intellect[17]

> The beginning of civilizations did not start abruptly, instead there was a gradual change from tribal society to civilized society; some changes did happen quickly, but others did not. Many civilizations had different characteristics than their neighbors, but there are seven common "building blocks" of civilization;

    I.   *a food surplus*

    II.   *cities*

    III.   *labor specialization*

    IV.   *religion ["opiate of the masses", you will get an even share at a later time]*

    V.   *social and economic organizations*

    VI.   *an organized government and*

    VII.   *a writing system [records of who owns what].[18]*

[16] Retrieved from: http://www.dictionary.com/browse/civilized
[17] Retrieved from: http://www.audioenglish.org/dictionary/animal_nature.htm
[18] Retrieved from: https://ridgeaphistory.wikispaces.com/Characteristics+of+Civilizations

What Does the Individual Gain from a Civilization?

I follow some statements from Sigmund Freud's view of civilization:

Is civilization a benefit or harm to human beings?....

The origins of civilization are in the individual. Each of us is born into a threatening world and we seek to avoid pain and gain pleasure. Thus, on Freud's view, the birth of civilization is rooted in egoism -- each of us striving in an often hostile world, to create the greatest amount of personal happiness and avoid pain as best we can....

As Freud sees the evolutionary development of human beings, early people strove to survive in a difficult and harsh world where there were three distinct sources of danger:

- Danger that the external world posed and in which we had to carve our survival. This would include not only such things as floods, storms and earthquakes, but many other factors such as extreme cold, extreme heat, the danger of other non-living creatures, diseases, and such items.
- Danger that came from our weak bodies that allowed us to get sick and always, eventually, to die.
- Danger that came from other human beings.

... Freud picks up human being at a much later time in evolutionary development when in fact the first two problems have been faced and incredible progress has been made precisely because human being has entered into civilization. Civilization is a relationship among individuals in which individuals give up certain aspects of their own ego interests to join with other people in creating social institutions which address the first two dangers, and to some extent the third as well.

However, this dependence-creating union carries new dangers of its own, since the social structures of civilization demand many limits on the individual which clash with fundamental and very deep evolutionary instincts....

Thus the community grows and each of us becomes deeply dependant [sic] upon it at many levels. However, in order to live together in community each of us is forced to deny some of the basic and fundamental instincts of being loved, having security and being able to act upon our aggressive desires.

What happens is that in order to make this change we unconsciously shift the nature of these desires, essentially lying to ourselves at some very deep level.

This is done by a process of sublimation, or convincing ourselves that our desires are other than they are....

He [Freud] is convinced that civilization asks much too much, demands rules it does not need for any reasonable sense of security....

He generally asserts that clearly civilization demands too much and this excess is likely to constitute a great deal of unhappiness in many people living in it. But, when all is said and done -- would it be better for humans to leave civilization and return to some pre-social state of nature. Probably not suspects Freud. However, neither is it at all likely that we will find a perfect balance and create a society where all will live in perfect harmony. No. This conflict between the individual's deepest instincts and the structures of any social system of civilization that we are likely to encounter will never be fully resolved. Civilization will attempt to oppress the individual into its needs and the individual will never have full happiness because of this. Some will have much more unhappiness than others, but civilization is by its fundamental nature incompatible at some levels with the individuals [sic] needs. [19]

---

[19] *Civilization and Its Discontents*, Sigmund Freud (1961).

CHAPTER 4: HOW HAVE OUR ANCESTORS SCORED IN PROGRESSING TO BEING CIVILIZED?

Let's set up an "Is Civilized" score card.

It will be based upon selected criteria from the previous chapter, and scored by how citizens feel about or experience the items:

Citizens Experience As ...

0 = Non-issue
-1 = An Issue
-2 = A Serious Issue

Granted, this will be biased, and granted it contains some modern elements because I want to rate the United Sates on the same score card in the last chapter. Proposed scored issues:

Adequate food (barring Nature's interventions)
Repression of animal savagery
Fear from harm from outside the community
Fear from harm from inside the community
Acceptance of authority and class structure
Stable government
Crime rate
Fair justice system
Adequate control of Nature & Human behavior

I will mostly focus upon Western Culture because I know it best.

However, other Culture Histories are mentioned. Each culture develops along basic lines, with advances and regressions.

These progressions and regressions will be plotted for various ancient civilizations later in the book.

Hunter-Gatherer Age

A hunter-gatherer is a human living in a society in which most or all food is obtained by foraging (collecting wild plants and pursuing wild animals), in contrast to agricultural societies, which rely mainly on domesticated species.

Hunting and gathering was humanity's first and most successful adaptation, occupying at least 90 percent of human history. Following the invention of agriculture, hunter-gatherers have been displaced or conquered by farming or pastoralist groups in most parts of the world.

Only a few contemporary societies are classified as hunter-gatherers, and many supplement their foraging activity with horticulture and/or keeping animals.[20]

And

During the twentieth century, anthropologists discovered and studied dozens of different hunter-gatherer societies, in various remote parts of the world, who had been nearly untouched by modern influences. Wherever they were found--in Africa, Asia, South America, or elsewhere; in deserts or in jungles--these societies had many characteristics in common. The people lived in small bands, of about 20 to 50 persons (including children) per band, who moved from camp to camp within a relatively circumscribed area to follow the available game and edible vegetation. The people had friends and relatives in neighboring bands and maintained peaceful relationships with neighboring bands. *Warfare was unknown* [italics mine] to most of these societies, and where it was known it was the result of interactions with warlike groups of people who were not hunter-gatherers. In each of these societies, *the dominant cultural ethos was one that emphasized individual autonomy,*

---

[20] Retrieved from: https://en.wikipedia.org/wiki/Hunter-gatherer

non-directive childrearing methods, nonviolence, sharing, cooperation, and consensual decision-making. Their core value, which underlay all of the rest, was that of the equality of individuals. [Italics mine][21]

Hunter-gatherers were egalitarian. A large animal has more meat than one family can eat. A hunter loses nothing by giving away the extra meat to other families. When the hunter comes home empty-handed, he can expect other men to share their kills. Because hunter-gatherers can't store meat, they measure wealth by social connections

Hunter-gatherers couldn't accumulate wealth. They couldn't store food. They didn't build permanent houses. Each person owned only what he could carry.

With nothing to steal, violence was minimal and warfare nonexistent [italics mine].

Men and women were equally responsible for producing food. They had equal status in hunter-gatherer societies. Hunter-gatherer societies have fixed gender roles, but everyone learns all basic skills for survival.

Each individual had equal opportunities to speak to the group. Each individual made his own decisions. A band that disagreed about a decision could split into two groups....

Most hunter-gatherers were monogamous. Most hunters could provide only enough meat for one wife and her children. The best hunters could support two wives (polygyny). -- Wikipedia

---

[21] Retrieved from: https://www.psychologytoday.com/blog/freedom-learn/201105/how-hunter-gatherers-maintained-their-egalitarian-ways

SCORE	ISSUE
0	Adequate food (barring Nature's interventions)
0	Repression of animal savagery
-1	Fear from harm from outside the community
0	Fear from harm from inside the community
0	Acceptance of authority and class structure
0	Stable government
0	Crime rate
0	Fair justice system
-1	Adequate control of Nature & Human behavior

Paleolithic Age

The Paleolithic ... Age, Era or Period is a prehistoric period of human history distinguished by the development of the most primitive stone tools discovered (Grahame Clark's Modes I and II), and covers roughly 95% of human *technological* [emphasis mine] prehistory. It extends from the earliest known use of stone tools, probably by Homo habilis initially, 2.6 million years ago, to the end of the Pleistocene around 10,000 BP [before present].

Humankind gradually evolved from early members of the genus *Homo* such as *Homo habilis* – who used simple stone tools – into fully behaviorally and anatomically modern humans (*Homo sapiens*) during the Paleolithic era. During the end of the Paleolithic, specifically the Middle and or Upper Paleolithic, humans began to produce the earliest works of art and engage in religious and spiritual behavior such as burial and ritual. The climate during the Paleolithic consisted of a set of glacial and interglacial periods in which the climate periodically fluctuated between warm and cool temperatures. Archaeological and genetic data suggest that the source populations of Paleolithic humans survived in sparsely wooded areas and dispersed through areas of high primary productivity while avoiding dense forest cover.

Similarly, scientists disagree whether Lower Paleolithic humans were largely monogamous or polygynous. In particular, the Provisional model suggests that bipedalism arose in Pre Paleolithic australopithecine societies as an adaptation to monogamous lifestyles; however, other researchers note that sexual dimorphism is more pronounced in Lower Paleolithic humans such as *Homo erectus* than in Modern humans, who are less polygynous than other primates, which suggests that Lower Paleolithic humans had a largely polygynous lifestyle, because species that have the most pronounced sexual dimorphism tend more likely to be polygynous.

Human societies from the Paleolithic to the early Neolithic farming tribes lived without states and organized governments. For most of the Lower Paleolithic, human societies were possibly more hierarchical than their Middle and Upper Paleolithic descendants, and probably were not grouped into bands, though during the end of the Lower Paleolithic, the latest populations of the hominid *Homo erectus* may have begun living in small-scale (possibly egalitarian) bands similar to both Middle and Upper Paleolithic societies and modern hunter-gatherers. – Wikipedia

SCORE	ISSUE
0	Adequate food (barring Nature's interventions)
0	Repression of animal savagery
-1	Fear from harm from outside the community
0	Fear from harm from inside the community
0	Acceptance of authority and class structure
0	Stable government
0	Crime rate
0	Fair justice system
-1	Adequate control of Nature & Human behavior

The Roman Empire

The Roman Empire ... was the post-Roman Republic period of the ancient Roman civilization, characterized by government headed by emperors and large territorial holdings around the Mediterranean Sea in Europe, Africa and Asia. The extended city of Rome was the largest city in the world c. 100 BC – c. 400 AD, with Constantinople (New Rome) becoming the largest around 500 AD, and the Empire's populace grew to an estimated 50 to 90 million inhabitants (roughly 20% of the world's population at the time). The 500-year-old republic which preceded it was severely destabilized in a series of civil wars and political conflict, during which Julius Caesar was appointed as perpetual dictator and then assassinated in 44 BC. Civil wars and executions continued, culminating in the victory of Octavian, Caesar's adopted son, over Mark Antony and Cleopatra at the Battle of Actium in 31 BC and the annexation of Egypt. Octavian's power was now unassailable and in 27 BC the Roman Senate formally granted him overarching power and the new title *Augustus*, effectively marking the end of the Roman Republic.

The imperial successor to the republic lasted approximately 1400 years....

The Roman Empire was among the most powerful economic, cultural, political and military forces in the world of its time. It was the largest empire of the classical antiquity period, and one of the largest empires in world history. At its height under Trajan, it covered 5 million square kilometers and held sway over some 70 million people, at that time 21% of the world's entire population. The longevity and vast extent of the empire ensured the lasting influence of Latin and Greek language, culture, religion, inventions, architecture, philosophy, law and forms of government on the empire's descendants. Throughout the European medieval period, attempts were even made to establish successors to the Roman Empire, including the Crusader state, the Empire of Romania and the Holy Roman

Empire. By means of European expansionism through the Spanish, French, Portuguese, Dutch, Italian, Russian, German, British and Belgian empires, Greco-Roman culture was spread on a worldwide scale, playing a significant role in the development of the modern world....

Rome had begun expanding shortly after the founding of the republic in the 6th century BC, though it did not expand outside Italy until the 3rd century BC. Then, it was an "empire" long before it had an emperor. *The Roman Republic was not a nation-state in the modern sense, but a network of towns left to rule themselves (though with varying degrees of independence from the Roman Senate) and provinces administered by military commanders* [italics mine]. It was ruled, not by emperors, but by annually elected magistrates (Roman Consuls above all) in conjunction with the senate. For various reasons, the 1st century BC was a time of political and military upheaval, which ultimately led to rule by emperors. The consuls' military power rested in the Roman legal concept of *imperium*, which literally means "command" (though typically in a military sense). Occasionally, successful consuls were given the honorary title *imperator* (commander), and this is the origin of the word *emperor* (and *empire*) since this title (among others) was always bestowed to the early emperors upon their accession. -- Wikipedia

Crime and Punishment

Not much has been written about punishments of the lower class folk. *Crimes such as false witness, adultery and counterfeiting were punished with the death penalty* [italics mine]. Less serious crimes were punished in a policy of "an eye for an eye". The death penalty was enforced by burying alive, throwing from a cliff or burning the guilty one. Executions were even ordered for possession of weapons with criminal intent or for possession of poison. *Such strict punishment was generally only enforced on criminals of the lower class. Members of the senatorial and equestrian classes were generally exiled for a given time (food and water forbidden within a given distance of Rome) and their property confiscated. Plebeians were scourged or sent to work in the mines* [italics mine]. During the empire, one could also choose to be sent to the arena. Since scourging and working in the mines often meant a slow lingering death, the choice of the games seemed a kinder solution to some. There is contradictory evidence of whether a citizen could be given a death penalty but, in effect, many of the punishments that members of the lower classes received were a sentence to death. Perhaps the biggest difference between Roman and contemporary legal systems is the use of prisons. Roman prisons were not used to punish criminals. Instead they served only to hold people awaiting trial or execution. Those who disobeyed court magistrates could also be imprisoned. The wealthy were generally held in house arrest at the home of a friend who would guarantee their presence at the trial. Private prisons existed for slaves.[22]

And

Some sexual attitudes and behaviors in ancient Roman culture differ markedly from those in later Western societies. Roman religion promoted sexuality as an aspect of prosperity for the state, and individuals might turn to private religious practice or "magic" for improving their erotic lives or reproductive health. Prostitution was legal, public, and widespread. "Pornographic" paintings were featured among the art collections in respectable upper class households. *It was considered natural and unremarkable for men to be sexually attracted to teen-aged youths of both sexes, and pederasty was condoned as long as the younger male partner was not a freeborn Roman* [italics mine] "Homosexual" and "heterosexual" did not form the primary dichotomy of Roman thinking about sexuality, and no Latin words for these concepts exist. No moral censure was directed at the man who enjoyed sex acts with either women or males of inferior status, as long as his behaviors revealed no

[22] Retrieved from: http://www.dl.ket.org/latin2/mores/legallatin/legal01.htm

weaknesses or excesses, nor infringed on the rights and prerogatives of his masculine peers. -- Wikipedia

Regressions to Animal Heritage

- The alpha structure of animals became prevalent over the individual freedoms of past eras.

- Class structure became pronounced.

- A legal system was imposed, with cruel punishments for small crimes, and the death penalty for greater crimes. The implementation of the law was dependent upon class.

- Monogamy and polygyny were replaced by the more natural promiscuity of many species of animals.

- Bands or groups of individuals in cities were ruled by a military commander.

Accommodations in Writings of the Dominant Religion to Conform to Common Civil Practice

In the early Middle Ages, Christianity was the preferred religion. Regarding homosexuality:

> In the New Testament (NT) there are at least three passages that may refer to homosexual activity: Romans 1:26–27, 1 Corinthians 6:9–10[23], and 1 Timothy 1:9–10[24]. A fourth passage, Jude 1:7, is often interpreted as referring to homosexuality.

---

[23] Forbidden, but a lower class sin: "Do you not know that the unrighteous will not inherit the kingdom of God? Do not be deceived. Neither fornicators, nor idolaters, nor adulterers, nor homosexuals, nor sodomites, nor thieves, nor covetous, nor drunkards, nor revilers, nor extortioners will inherit the kingdom of God."

[24] Same as above: knowing this: that the law is not made for a righteous person, but for *the* lawless and insubordinate, for *the* ungodly and for sinners, for *the* unholy and profane, for murderers of fathers and murderers of mothers, for manslayers, [10] for fornicators, for sodomites, for kidnappers, for liars, for perjurers, and if there is any other thing that is [3]contrary to sound doctrine"

None of the four gospels mentions the subject directly, and there is nothing about homosexuality in the Book of Acts, in Hebrews, in Revelation, or in the letters attributed to James, Peter, and John." – Wikipedia

But homosexual acts, although discouraged, were now classed as offenses equivalent to: liars, adulterers, murders, kidnappers, drunkenness, greed, etc.

Church and State have always been bedpartners [pun mine]. For mutual protection of institutions and civil order, and for the State to use the Church to carry its pronouncements.

SCORE	ISSUE
-1	Adequate food (barring Nature's interventions)
-2	Repression of animal savagery
0	Fear from harm from outside the community
-1	Fear from harm from inside the community
-2	Acceptance of authority and class structure
-2	Stable government
-1	Crime rate
-2	Fair justice system
0	Adequate control of Nature & Human behavior

The Middle Ages

In the history of Europe, the Middle Ages or medieval period lasted from the 5th to the 15th century. It began with the fall of the Western Roman Empire and merged into the Renaissance and the Age of Discovery....

Depopulation, deurbanization [sic], invasion, and movement of peoples, which had begun in Late Antiquity, continued in the Early Middle Ages. The barbarian invaders, including various Germanic peoples, formed new kingdoms in what remained of the Western Roman Empire. In the 7th century, North Africa and the Middle East—once part of the Eastern Roman Empire—came under the rule of the Umayyad Caliphate, an Islamic empire, after conquest by Muhammad's successors. Although there were substantial changes in society and political structures, the break with Antiquity was not complete.

The still-sizeable Byzantine Empire survived in the east and remained a major power. The empire's law code, the Corpus Juris Civilis or "Code of Justinian", was rediscovered in Northern Italy in 1070 and became widely admired later in the Middle Ages....

During the High Middle Ages, which began after 1000, the population of Europe increased greatly as technological and agricultural innovations allowed trade to flourish and the Medieval Warm Period climate change allowed crop yields to increase. *Manorialism, the organisation of peasants into villages that owed rent and labour services to the nobles* [italics mine], and feudalism, the political structure whereby knights and lower-status nobles owed military service to their overlords in return for the right to rent from lands and manors, were two of the ways society was organised in the High Middle Ages. – Wikipedia

Middle Ages Crime

During the Middle Ages, crimes were very common. This was caused because of impunity among other reasons which caused burglars and thieves exert more frequently their activities. Of course, education also played a primary role in this as most burglars had no education at all and thus; instead of working they would simply resort to steal.

Punishment for thieves varied greatly. Medieval torture was used mostly even if the thief only stole bread to feed himself. Of course death to thieves very rarely happened and they were just publicly tortured.

Nevertheless, different kingdoms had different ways to punish criminals. As a brief example, Vlad the Impaler (AKA Dracula) was famous for impaling criminals even if the only thing they stole was bread.

For most of Western Europe, stealing was punished by torture as I mentioned above. However there were different punishments for different crimes. Unfaithful wives were considered to be criminals and they would be treated accordingly. Witches were considered to be criminals as well and heresy was one of the greatest crimes.

Imprisonment happened very frequently and sometimes inside a prison there were torture chambers to further teach people that crimes were not good [italics mine].

Some kings who were especially obsessed with their kingdom's honesty, attempted to capture every criminal. If a criminal got away with a crime, some kings went to the nearest village to kill people out of spite.

Kidnapping was very frequent during the Dark Ages. *This was mostly done by foreign invaders who needed kids to work their own lands. Landlords who lacked enough workers, frequently resorted to kidnapping kids in order to populate their own villages* [emphasis mine]. Punishment for these crimes were of a very high magnitude and if the kid was part of the royalty, the offender would be heavily tortured and executed in a public plaza.

Most crimes did occur to merchants. Merchants who traveled alone during the Dark Ages were very prone to such attacks. Even when merchants traveled together, they were still in danger of a large group of enemies to attack and rob them.

Most kingdoms were skeptic about this and imposed heavy penalties to captured thieves. This led to much Medieval

Folklore - including the legend of Robin Hood among others.

It was during the Inquisition when criminals were heavily tortured. The most common ways to torture or execute criminals during the Inquisition was by Burning at the Stake, using The Wheel Torture, using the Head Vice Torture among others.

This, of course, helped combat criminals because during the Earlier Medieval Times, when there was much impunity, more crimes took place. Later on, when fear was inspired in the average peasant, crimes lowered considerably.

It was common for a town to express its anger against a thief by hanging him in public. When the Guillotine was introduced into medieval Europe, it was quickly used for executing criminals.

Crimes were, for the most part, done by the poor.

Nevertheless, there are records of nobles and knights being hanged for robbing.

Rape was not considered a major offense because women had not as many rights as men. Nevertheless, it was a crime to marry a relative as it was strictly forbidden by the church.

For kings and high nobles, punishment was almost non-existant. They could practically get away with raping, abusing, etc. Kings even had a right to stay in whichever house they pleased and sleep with whichever woman they wanted to because they were "appointed by God." Unfortunately, punishment was mostly reserved for the poor.[25]

---

[25] Retrieved from: http://medieval-castles.org/index.php/medieval_crimes_thieves_burglars_kidnapp

Male Sexuality

In the early part of the Middle ages, soldiers were encouraged to form male-male couples.

> Homosexuality in the militaries of ancient Greece was regarded as contributing to morale. Although the primary example is the Sacred Band of Thebes, a unit said to have been formed of same-sex couples, the Spartan tradition of military heroism has also been explained in light of strong emotional bonds resulting from homosexual relationships. Various ancient Greek sources record incidents of courage in battle and interpret them as motivated by homoerotic bonds. – Wikipedia

Female Sexuality

> ... Like a modern woman, a medieval woman's sexuality included many different aspects. Sexuality not only included sex, but spread into many parts of the medieval woman's life.

> Everything in her life ultimately led to marriage, and it was within wedlock that her sexuality developed and took shape into what today could be recognized as a sexual identity. The scope of sexuality for a married woman during the Middle Ages was broader than that of an unmarried woman. While there are many reasons for this, an important one is that the Church only acknowledged the potential for a sexual identity in a woman partaking in sexual intercourse with her husband alone.

> Outside of marriage, virginity and purity were prized, and sexuality was limited to small displays of beauty, such as embroidered hair coverings or fine clothes. Chastity removed the possibility for any kind of sexual identity as would be seen in the 21st century.

> Even medical problems related to female organs were disregarded with the understanding that only sexually active

women [within matrimony] could have them, and even so, help was difficult to find .... Those problems included conception, birthing, abortion, and health problems related to sexual organs.

The most important piece of a woman's sexuality did not directly relate to what women believed about their own sexuality, but more so the roles assigned to them through the beliefs, superstitions, and decrees of the Church, the law, and men. These three entities came to define female sexuality and sexual identity in the Middle Ages. – Wikipedia

Side Issue: Sexually Transmitted Disease

As human populations grew larger, the villages became so large that sexual indiscretions could become discrete. The number of indiscretions increased, and turned into a mass-killer.

The first well-recorded European outbreak of what is now known as syphilis occurred in 1494 when it broke out among French troops besieging Naples in the Italian War of 1494–98. The disease may have originated from the Columbian Exchange. From Naples, the disease swept across Europe, killing more than five million people. As Jared Diamond describes it, "[W]hen syphilis was first definitely recorded in Europe in 1495, its pustules often covered the body from the head to the knees, caused flesh to fall from people's faces, and led to death within a few months," rendering it far more fatal than it is today. Diamond concludes,"[B]y 1546, the disease had evolved into the disease with the symptoms so well known to us today." Gonorrhoeae is recorded at least up to 700 years ago and associated with a district in Paris formerly known as "Le Clapiers". This is where the prostitutes were to be found at that time." – Wikipedia

Control of The Birth Canal: Accommodation to STD's, As Well As to the Need for a Steady Stream of Males for Farm Work and for War

- Women's equality was eroded for three reasons involving controlling the birth canal:

  Sexually transmitted disease
  Farm animals became expensive, so they were replaced by large numbers of children
  Soldiers were in constant demand to fight territorial wars, and casualties were large.

- Women's rights diminished greatly, they became property of a husband, and were strictly controlled.

- Similarly, homosexuality was severely outlawed. Same-sex couple don't produce farm animals and soldiers.

- Again, I believe health issues, political issues, and war issues crept into religious doctrine and writings. Church degraded the roles of women to maintain control of their unique capability: birth.

SCORE	ISSUE
-2	Adequate food (barring Nature's interventions)
-2	Repression of animal savagery
-2	Fear from harm from outside the community
-1	Fear from harm from inside the community
-2	Acceptance of authority and class structure
-2	Stable government
-2	Crime rate
-2	Fair justice system
-1	Adequate control of Nature & Human behavior

The Renaissance

The Renaissance ... is a period in Europe, from the 14th to the 17th century, considered the bridge between the Middle Ages and modern history. It started as a cultural movement in Italy in the Late Medieval period and later spread to the rest of Europe, marking the beginning of the Early Modern Age.

The Renaissance's intellectual basis was its own invented version of humanism[26], derived from the rediscovery of classical Greek philosophy, such as that of Protagoras, who said, that 'Man is the measure of all things.' This new thinking became manifest in art, architecture, politics, science and literature. Early examples were the development of *perspective* in oil painting and the recycled knowledge of how to make concrete. Although the invention of metal movable [printing] type sped the dissemination of ideas from the later 15th century, the changes of the Renaissance were not uniformly experienced across Europe.... – Wikipedia

Crime

The Renaissance is considered the rebirth after the middle ages, which was known for its various types of torture. Though the Renaissance was not as cruel, the penalty for crimes are still considered one of the harshest in history.

The punishment for an individual depended upon their social standing. Most of the crimes committed by the lower class were out of a necessity to survive.

During this time, the effects of the Black Death were starting to die down and the population was slowly recovering. Later on, there was an overpopulation of people in certain cities, which

[26] The humanists believed that it is important to transcend to the afterlife with a perfect mind and body. This transcending belief can be done with education. The purpose of humanism was to create a universal man whose person combined intellectual and physical excellence and who was capable of functioning honorably in virtually any situation.

left a number of people without work. Because of this their [sic] were people left starving and desperate enough to steal. Theft during this time was an everyday occurrence. Any citizen who stole anything worth more than 5 pence would be hanged.

Those who did not steal would resort to poaching. Hunting was a right reserved for the upper class and anyone caught poaching were liable to be hanged, castrated, or blinded. In the more severe cases the peasant would be sewn into a deer skin and then hunted down by dogs.

Those who relied on other people's charity were not safe either. Begging was taken as a serious crime and dealt with harshly. Whoever was caught begging would be relentlessly beaten until they reached the town parish border. For those people who were continuously caught for begging, they would be either sentenced to prison or hanged.

Other common crimes included:
- Debtors
- Cut purses[27]
- Forgery
- Adultery

The punishment for the nobility was a slightly different matter. Those who caught were mostly condemned to the guillotine. Instead of a public execution, they were done in private where the rich exclusively saw the execution.

These crimes included:

- Blasphemy
- High Treason
- Spying
- Rebellion[28]

---

[27] Pick pockets
[28] Retrieved from: http://crimeintherenaissance.weebly.com/

Humanism is a philosophical and ethical stance that emphasizes the value and agency of human beings, individually and collectively, and generally prefers critical thinking and evidence (rationalism, empiricism) over acceptance of dogma or superstition. The meaning of the term *humanism* has fluctuated according to the successive intellectual movements which have identified with it....

-Ancient South Asia-

Human-centered philosophy that rejected the supernatural can be found also circa 1500 BCE in the Lokayata system of Indian philosophy. Nasadiya Sukta, a passage in the Rig Veda, contains one of the first recorded assertion of agnosticism. In the 6th-century BCE, Gautama Buddha expressed, in Pali literature, a skeptical attitude toward the supernatural ....

Another instance of ancient humanism as an organised system of thought is found in the Gathas of Zarathustra, composed between 1,000 BCE – 600 BCE in Greater Iran. Zarathustra's philosophy in the Gathas lays out a conception of humankind as thinking beings dignified with choice and agency according to the intellect which each receives from Ahura Mazda (God in the form of supreme wisdom). The idea of Ahura Mazda as a non-intervening deistic divine God/Grand Architect of the universe tied with a unique eschatology and ethical system implying that each person is held morally responsible for their choices, made freely in this present life, in the afterlife. The importance placed on thought, action, responsibility, and a non-intervening creator was appealed to by, and inspired a number of, Enlightenment humanist thinkers in Europe such as Voltaire and Montesquieu.

-Ancient China-

In China, Yellow Emperor is regarded as the humanistic primogenitor. Sage kings such as Yao and Shun are humanistic

45

figures as recorded. King Wu of Zhou has the famous saying: "Humanity is the Ling (efficacious essence) of the world (among all)." Among them Duke of Zhou, respected as a founder of Rujia (Confucianism), is especially prominent and pioneering in humanistic thought. His words were recorded in the *Book of History* ....

Heaven (or "God") is not believable. Our Tao (special term referring to "the way of nature") includes morality (derived from the philosophy of former sage kings and to be continued forward).

In the 6th century BCE, Taoist teacher Lao Tzu espoused a series of naturalistic concepts with some elements of humanistic philosophy. The Silver Rule of Confucianism from *Analects* XV.24, is an example of ethical philosophy based on human values rather than the supernatural. Humanistic thought is also contained in other Confucian classics, e.g., as recorded in Zuo Zhuan, Ji Liang says, "People is the zhu (master, lord, dominance, owner or origin) of gods. So, to sage kings, people first, gods second"; Neishi Guo says, "Gods, clever, righteous and wholehearted, comply with human." Taoist and Confucian secularism contain elements of moral thought devoid of religious authority or deism however they only partly resembled our modern concept of secularism.

-Ancient Greece-

6th-century BCE pre-Socratic Greek philosophers Thales of Miletus and Xenophanes of Colophon were the first in the region to attempt to explain the world in terms of human reason rather than myth and tradition, thus can be said to be the first Greek humanists. Thales questioned the notion of anthropomorphic gods and Xenophanes refused to recognise [sic] the gods of his time and reserved the divine for the principle of unity in the universe. These Ionian Greeks were the first thinkers to assert that nature is available to be studied separately from the supernatural realm. Anaxagoras brought philosophy and the spirit of rational inquiry from Ionia to Athens. Pericles, the leader of Athens during the period of its greatest glory was an admirer of Anaxagoras. Other influential pre-Socratics or rational philosophers include Protagoras (like Anaxagoras a friend of Pericles), known for his famous dictum "man is the measure of all things" and Democritus, who proposed that matter was composed of atoms. Little of the written work of these early philosophers survives and they are known mainly from fragments and quotations in other writers, principally Plato and Aristotle. The historian Thucydides, noted for his scientific and rational approach to history, is also much admired by later humanists. In the 3rd century BCE, Epicurus became known for his concise phrasing of the problem of evil, lack of belief in the afterlife, and human-centered approaches to achieving eudaimonia. He was also the first Greek philosopher to admit women to his school as a rule.

-Medieval Islam-

Many medieval Muslim thinkers pursued humanistic, rational and scientific discourses in their search for knowledge, meaning and values. A wide range of Islamic writings on love, poetry, history and philosophical theology show that medieval Islamic thought was open to the humanistic ideas of individualism, occasional secularism, skepticism, and liberalism.

According to Imad-ad-Dean Ahmad, another reason the Islamic world flourished during the Middle Ages was an early emphasis on freedom of speech, as summarised [sic] by al-Hashimi (a cousin of Caliph al-Ma'mun) in the following letter to one of the religious opponents he was attempting to convert through reason:

Bring forward all the arguments you wish and say whatever you please and speak your mind freely. Now that you are safe and free to say whatever you please appoint some arbitrator who will impartially judge between us and lean only towards the truth and be free from the empery of passion, and that arbitrator shall be Reason, whereby God makes us responsible for our own rewards and punishments. Herein I have dealt justly with you and have given you full security and am ready to accept whatever decision Reason may give for me or against me. For "There is no compulsion in religion" (Qur'an 2:256) and I have only invited you to accept our faith willingly and of your own accord and have pointed out the hideousness of your present belief. Peace be with you and the blessings of God. – Wikipedia

Accomplishments!

This was the beginning of repudiation of the animal heritage in human culture. Humans were considered "higher" than animals, closer to the deity.

The Renaissance was a discovery of the uniqueness, and the break with the past foundations of *Homo sapiens*.

SCORE	ISSUE
-1	Adequate food (barring Nature's interventions)
0	Repression of animal savagery
-1	Fear from harm from outside the community
0	Fear from harm from inside the community
-1	Acceptance of authority and class structure
-1	Stable government
-1	Crime rate
-1	Fair justice system
-1	Adequate control of Nature & Human behavior

CHAPTER 5: ISSUES AND PROBLEMS UNIQUE TO THE HUMAN ANIMAL

Unique Human Needs Not Common with Animals

Humans, because they are self-aware and understand death, have several "needs" that are filled from the external, to maintain an internal balanced mental life:[29]

> The Need for Affection and Approval
> The Need to Restrict One's Life within Narrow Borders
> The Need for Prestige
> The Need for Personal Admiration
> The Need for Personal Achievement
> The Need for Self-Sufficiency and Independence.

However, when one "needs" more than is necessary, it becomes a neurotic need (Merriam Webster Dictionary: often or always fearful or worried about something; tending to worry in a way that is not healthy or reasonable).

Ask a psychologist, there is no such thing as "sane" or "not crazy"; we are all irrational concerning our "blind spots", or parts of our character we are not willing to acknowledge. And humans are incredibly good at hiding their blind spots from themselves!

Example: Most anyone would be willing to admit readily that they are not as tall as they wished. There is probably no way to change that.

However, to admit one is "controlling" would open the question of changing that behavior (considering its downside, alienation of companions). Indeed, being controlling has a payoff: being in control means not having to acknowledge an *unbalanced fear* of the environment.

---

[29] This is a subset of those listed below as Neuroses.

We are all neurotic (irrational), it is only a matter of degree.

Returning to our "needs" list above, a "need" may become imbalanced, resulting in abnormal fear or anxiety; in addition, there are several neuroses that are not related to "absolute needs", they are purely irrational attempts to maintain mind balance (labeled * below).

The <u>neuroses</u> unique to humans are:

- The *Neurotic* Need for Affection and Approval
- The *Neurotic* Need for a Partner Who Will Take Over One's Life*
- The *Neurotic* Need to Restrict One's Life within Narrow Borders
- The *Neurotic* Need for Power*
- The *Neurotic* Need to Exploit Others*
- The *Neurotic* Need for Prestige
- The *Neurotic* Need for Personal Admiration
- The *Neurotic* Need for Personal Achievement
- The *Neurotic* Need for Self-Sufficiency and Independence
- The *Neurotic* Need for Perfection and Unassailability*.[30]

I will add three more Human *Neuroses*:

- Excitement*.

As will be pointed out later in this book, contemporary individuals have become addicted to their own adrenaline, and need increasing levels of stimulation, general excitement, and horror.

- *Psychopathy*.

> **Antisocial personality disorder** (also known as dissocial personality disorder, psychopathy, and sociopathy) is a personality disorder, characterized by a pervasive pattern of disregard for, or violation of, the rights of others. An

---

[30] Retrieved from: http://psychology.about.com/od/theoriesofpersonality/a/neuroticneeds.htm

impoverished moral sense or conscience is often apparent, as well as a history of crime, legal problems, and/or impulsive and aggressive behavior. -- Wikipedia

[Diagnosis involves identifying] three or more of the following:

1. failure to conform to social norms with respect to lawful behaviors as indicated by repeatedly performing acts that are grounds for arrest;
2. deception, as indicated by repeatedly lying, use of aliases, or conning others for personal profit or pleasure;
3. impulsivity or failure to plan ahead;
4. irritability and aggressiveness, as indicated by repeated physical fights or assaults;
5. reckless disregard for safety of self or others;
6. consistent irresponsibility, as indicated by repeated failure to sustain consistent work behavior or honor financial obligations;
7. lack of remorse, as indicated by being indifferent to or rationalizing having hurt, mistreated, or stolen from another. – Wikipedia

Note, these people are not necessarily axe-murderers, although some are. They are just the people who:

Wheel a heaping shopping cart into a "Speedy Check Out, 20 items or less". Or block the aisle in a grocery store sideways so no one can pass and wander bleary-eyed up and down the aisle.

Are the 90% of the population who keeps the 10% (who actually get things done) in Hell.

Are called "self-absorbed", or the one I like, "center-of-the-Universe" people.

*****

According to Psychologists, the steps in the developing "perspective taking" [noticing other people in the world] are[31]:

> Despite differences in the research literature, there is agreement that awareness develops gradually from an egocentric perspective to the ability to respond to and even predict how others will feel…. Anyone working with young children is aware of their egocentricity…. According to Selman Hildebrandt, and Zan[32], with experience and guidance, people move through five levels of perspective taking as follows: Level 0, not recognizing that others have feelings or ideas different from your own, is common during preschool. During the primary grades, most children operate at level 1. At this point, young children realize that others have their own feelings, but can't consider someone else's feelings while thinking about their own. Our observation shows that this is particularly true when their own feelings are in opposition to the other person's. As they move into upper elementary school, level 2 thinking is more common. This brings the ability to consider another person's views as well as their own. Levels 3 and 4 bring increasing decentering and the ability to coordinate mutual perspectives. However, these generally do not emerge until adolescence and adulthood. Theory of mind research points out the role of maturation as children develop understanding of their own and others' thinking….

These descriptions reveal that there are unknown thousands of Americans wandering around who have not left adolescence psychologically nor in personality development, but by chronological age can drive and vote.

[31] Retrieved from: http://www.education.com/reference/article/learning-perspective-taking/
[32] DeVries, R., Hildebrandt, C., & Zan, B. (2000). Constructivist early education for moral development. *Early Education and Development, 11*(1), 9–35.

Downside: These people are prime bait for scam artists and politicians, and have mostly lost their civil rights as well as any control over their destinies.

Finally added,

• The need to convert the "bell-curve" population into an "all the same" one.*

This is an expansion of a prior mentioned neurotic need.

When considering any "dimension"[33] of the human animal, the concept of the "Normal" or "Bell" curve comes to mind. Most people center about some middle ground (say, average looks), and there are extremes" Hollywood stars and the grossly malformed.

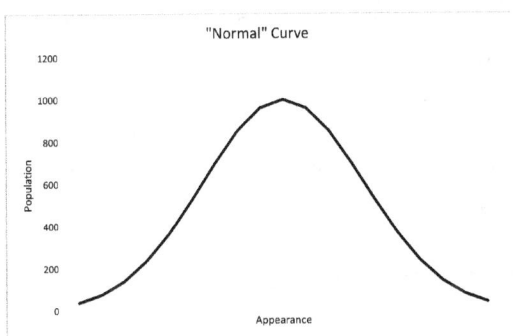

Since time began for humans, the need to be "normal" has caused humans to target and "kill off" the extremes, make all people the same. So that the majority that exists are all the same and all can feel comfortable.

---

[33] Beauty, intelligence, humor, sociability, etc.

"Flat" Curve

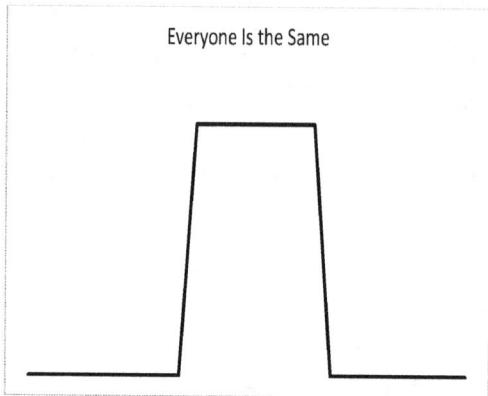

Everyone Is the Same

In America, until a hundred years ago or so, human parents on occasion killed their offspring routinely (NOT including post-partem depression issues). If there were too many children to feed, or if an ugly or deformed one were born, requirements-support, such as food, was withdrawn until death.

Some "extremes" such as intelligence, creativeness, and unwillingness to be "normal" cannot be detected in childhood.

When the adult "extremes" are vocal, problems may arise.

Especially totalitarian governments cannot tolerate the spot light these people shine on their behaviors, and they are killed or expelled from that society.

Examples: Nazi Germany (most of these people were Jews), Communist Countries, Dictatorships, Religious groups, etc.

As an example in the United States of marginalizing contrary views, there was a plank on a State of Texas party platform that proposed that "critical thinking" NOT be taught in Texas schools. One take on this is that these political leaders didn't want to face thinking voters, just sheep.

As pointed out in another book[34], America's public education system has been "normalized" to about 6th grade by parents and politicians, although for very different reasons.

Regarding US Politics

Especially in the 2016 Presidential primary election process, a common statement is, "If you don't like it here (the way we have rigged the system), leave!"

And we have forgotten that all of the Political Party ploys (caucuses, winner-take-all, delegates rather than actual votes, the electoral college, etc.) are historical strategies to keep the votes of "You know who!" from counting. Except this time, the "You know who!" is a very disenchanted, hostile, anti-establishment majority in 2016.

*****

Note that these personal neuroses are a setup for interpersonal competition and strife! One's neurotic need is often fulfilled at someone else's expense.

When one or more of these neuroses becomes completely out of control or extreme, we call this psychosis.[35]

Let's explore **psychosis**.

Neuroses, Psychoses and Violence

Violence is extremely common, violent crimes occurring literally in the hundreds of thousands every year. Individual's

---

[34] *The American Middle Class Is Being Reorganized*. C. E. Nough (2016).

[35] **Psychosis** refers to an abnormal condition of the mind described as involving a "loss of contact with reality". People with psychosis are described as *psychotic*. People experiencing psychosis may exhibit some personality changes and thought disorder. Depending on its severity, this may be accompanied by unusual or bizarre behavior, as well as difficulty with social interaction and impairment in carrying out daily life activities. -- Wikipedia

assault each other impulsively, almost casually, even those whom they love. The causes of violence are, consequently, the subject of much attention—especially now, in the wake of a number of mass shootings. Every time someone commits a violent act so egregious that it comes to public notice, a dozen reasons are given for it and for all acts of violence. Poverty is blamed, or prejudice, or overcrowding. But the truth is that the causes of violence are innumerable.

Mental illness is commonly alleged to be a principal cause for violent behavior. For that reason many uninformed people are frightened of someone who is obviously disturbed emotionally. Yet mental illness, like most physical illness, tends to impair the individual's ability to act, aggressively or in any other way. Only a few such conditions have a significant potential to precipitate a violent act. Among these is paranoid schizophrenia, which may affect the individual so that he comes to believe that people are persecuting him. He may then attack whomever he imagines his enemies to be. Certain drugs—for example, amphetamines—produce psychotic paranoid states which can be dangerous for the same reason. As everyone knows, alcoholic intoxication, because it lowers impulse control, causes some people to become violent; and if they are chronic alcoholics, they become violent over and over again.[36]

Stress Induced Psychosis

This article presents evidence suggesting that psychosocial stress may increase risk for psychosis, especially in the case of cumulative exposure. A heuristically useful framework to study the underlying mechanisms is the concept of "behavioral sensitization" that stipulates that exposure to psychosocial stress—such as life events, childhood trauma, or discriminatory experiences—may progressively increase the behavioral and

[36] Psychology Today. https://www.psychologytoday.com/blog/fighting-fear/201401/the-relationship-between-violence-and-psychotic-disorders

biological response to subsequent exposures."[37]

And

> There are many models, most of them stemming from the field of work and organizational psychology, that identify precursors of mental ill health. These precursors are often labelled "stressors". Those models differ in their scope and, related to this, in the number of stressor dimensions identified....
>
> A more elaborate model is that of Warr (1994), with nine dimensions: opportunity for control (~decision authority), opportunity for skill use (~skill discretion), externally generated goals (~quantitative and qualitative demands), variety, environmental clarity (information about consequences of behavior [sic], availability of feedback, information about the future, information about required behavior[sic]), availability of money, physical security (low physical risk, absence of danger), opportunity for interpersonal contact (~prerequisite for social support), and valued social position (cultural and company evaluations of status, personal evaluations of significance). From the above it is clear that the precursors of mental (ill) health are generally psychosocial in nature, and are related to work content, as well as working conditions, conditions of employment and (formal and informal) relationships at work.[38]

In the next chapter, we will explore the fact that the presence of psychosocial stressors has increased vastly in the past decade or so.

So when we say that people who go psychotic and commit mass murder are "crazy", I would ask, "Who made them crazy?" The answer will be

---

[37] Psychosocial stress and psychosis. Retrieved from:
http://www.ncbi.nlm.nih.gov/pubmed/18718885
[38] http://www.ilocis.org/documents/chpt5e.htm

"us".

Personally, I view humans as overbred for certain characteristics: self-awareness, rational thought, avoidance of environmental hazards, etc. But like Poodles are bred for certain characteristics, the cost has been "nervousness".

CHAPTER 6: HOW CIVILIZED IS THE UNITED STATES?

MY Examples of Mass Neuroses In America: Who Is Really "Crazy"?

- Wall Street brokers "needed" excitement (risk) and greed. Yet they have destroyed 1/3 of the World's wealth, and have pulled the safety nets out from under millions of Americans, as well as life-savings, and these have not been replaced.

- Parents and politicians and school boards (pawns of parents) "need" to control the form of education our children are delivered, and "feel" more capable than professional educators. Result: America's education system is circling the drain.

- America's ruling bodies "know" what people they have never met "need" (through mind reading), and legislate travesties follow.

- We "need" to reform criminals, but our prisons are extreme torture. We see the portrayal of prison life on Television and in the Movies, and are exceedingly glad it couldn't happen to us.

- We all "need" the most *recent* iphone, but the National Debt and the Trade Deficit will soon destroy America as we know it.

- We "need" to look like movie stars, but ill health results.

- We "need" to get married, but then 50% of us realize it was not a need.

- We "need" power, but then ruin lives of innocents around us.

- We "need" to exploit others, because of sloth or basic incompetence.

- We "need" to steal intellectual property because of incompetence and sloth.

- We "need" prestige, admiration, and achievement, but attain it by robbing others of their prestige, admiration, and achievement.

- We "need" to be safe, but don't support the safety of others. (Bankrupt retirement plans, limited access to healthcare, etc.).

  Example: Following the Great Recession, there were in Las Vegas, Nevada "Zombie Zones": whole neighborhoods where public services (Fire, Police, and Emergency services) were unavailable because of reduced public service budgets.

- We "need" excitement, so our entertainment becomes louder, gorier, and more violent. Never mind that our children are beginning to blur excitement and crime, and our people are getting hooked (addicted) to their own adrenaline.

- We "need" more excitement, so we take drugs.

- We "need" more tranquility, so we take drugs.

Every time we overdo our "needs", we pull the security net from under others and drive them closer to an "episode".

And we do this constantly, without let up.

When our victims lose control from the stress *we cause them*, we call them "crazy". But who, really, is "crazy"? **The one who acts out, or the ones who rode their ass until they broke?**

The Privileged Rich and Celebrities

America claims it is a Democracy.

> **Democracy**, or **democratic government**, is "a system of government in which all the people of a state or polity ... are involved in making decisions about its affairs, typically by voting to elect representatives to a parliament or similar assembly," as defined by the Oxford English Dictionary. Democracy is further defined as (a) government by the people, especially rule of the majority (b) a government in which the supreme power is vested in the people and exercised by them directly or indirectly through a system of representation usually involving periodically held free elections.

> According to political scientist Larry Diamond, it consists of four key elements: (a) A political system for choosing and replacing the government through free and fair elections; (b) The active participation of the people, as citizens, in politics and civic life; (c) Protection of the human rights of all citizens, and (d) A rule of law, in which the laws and procedures apply equally to all citizens. – Wikipedia

And

> The American system is *not* a democracy. It is a constitutional republic. A democracy, if you attach meaning to terms, is a system of unlimited majority rule; the classic example is ancient Athens. And the symbol of it is the fate of Socrates, who was put to death legally, because the majority didn't like what he was saying, although he had initiated no force and had violated no one's rights.

> Democracy, in short, is a form of collectivism, which denies individual rights: the majority can do whatever it wants with no restrictions. In principle, the democratic government is all-

powerful. Democracy is a totalitarian manifestation; it is not a form of freedom . . . .

The American system is a constitutionally limited republic, restricted to the protection of individual rights. In such a system, majority rule is applicable only to lesser details, such as the selection of certain personnel. But the majority has no say over the *basic* principles governing the government. It has no power to ask for or gain the infringement of individual rights.[39]

And

Man's rights can be violated only by the use of physical force. It is only by means of physical force that one man can deprive another of his life, or enslave him, or rob him, or prevent him from pursuing his own goals, or compel him to act against his own rational judgment." ... Rights derive from the mind's needs: for an organism that survives by means of reason, freedom is a survival-requirement: initiated force negates or paralyzes the thinking mind. Rand's overall argument is that rights protect freedom in order to protect reason. "Force and mind are opposites."[40]

And

The first Amendment highlights specific aspects of a free society by promising freedom of religion, speech, press, freedom to peaceably assemble, and a redress of grievances for its citizens. It forbids the government to infringe upon those rights and therefore limits the powers of the government so that the people of our democratic society can function without oppression. – Alexander Hamilton

---

[39] *Textbook of Americanism.* Ayn Rand.
[40] *The Virtue of Selfishness.* Ayn Rand.

Summing up, *American* Democracy (among other things) means freedom of the individual from loss of inalienable human rights via force from another individual, or from the government itself.

This part of Democracy is dependent upon the integrity of the Legal System, which in America is known *by all* to be faulty in these matters.

THEREFORE, IN MY OPINION, AMERICA IS NO LONGER A DEMOCRACY OR A REPUBLIC IN ANY FORM. THE UNITED STATES HAS TOTALLY GIVEN ITSELF OVER TO BASE ANIMAL BEHAVIORS.

Example: The "Justice" System:

> There are two criminal justice systems in the United States. One is for people with wealth, fame or influence who can afford to hire top-notch attorneys and public relations firms, who make campaign contributions to sheriffs, legislators and other elected officials, and who enjoy certain privileges due to their celebrity status or the size of their bank accounts. The other justice system is for everybody else.

> As one example of this dichotomy, for over a decade suburban jails in Southern California have been renting upscale cells to affluent people convicted of crimes in Los Angeles County. These pay-to-stay programs, also called self-pay jails, cost wealthy prisoners between $45 and $175 a day and include such amenities as iPods, cell phones, computers, private cells and work release programs. Some even let prisoners (who are referred to as "clients") bring in their own food.

> This nicer-jail-stay-for-pay scheme not only allows the rich and famous – as well as the more modestly affluent – to avoid the brutality, squalor, abysmal medical care and other unpleasant conditions typical in public jail systems. It also highlights the inequities of a two-track system of justice in the United States in which the wealthy enjoy privileges and perks behind bars while

the poor are resigned to less comfortable and more dangerous conditions of confinement.

The disparity in the U.S. criminal justice system begins with arrest. The poor are often arrested during SWAT-type raids in the middle of the night that leave their front doors, and possibly their entire homes, in a shambles. The affluent are frequently allowed to "turn themselves in," usually accompanied by their attorney. This assumes that people with means and influence are arrested in the first place, of course.[41]

And

There are 17 Hollywood Celebrities *alleged* to have received preferential treatment in cases involved with death. A few listed are:

Ted Kennedy
Michael Masse
Donte Stallworth
Robert Blake
Fatty Arbuckle
Laura Bush, etc.[42]

The reader can look at the circumstances of each and decide for themselves. No one can absolutely prove the punishments were for true crimes nor unjust.

The Entitled Millennial Generation

The Millennial Generation has been seriously programmed (by American Civilization) with ideas that do not represent the world millennials are entering, such as:

---

[41] Prison Legal News. Matt Clark. March 24, 2016.

[42] http://listabuzz.com/17-famous-people-who-probably-murdered-people-and-got-away-with-it/

a. America can continue grow indefinitely, with Americans living on a continuing Ponzi scheme of profits

b. The "good life" of their parents continues in an ongoing way to be available to them

c. Buy now, pay later will work indefinitely

d. Technology and Gadgets and Entertainment are inalienable perks of American living

e. They are entitled to an easy, high-paying job without the grungy work their parents did to secure such positions

f. That Millennials are special, and deserve naturally (are entitled to) the best of everything: easy-education, houses, leisure time, movie-star-like mates, etc.

g. There are no problems on the American horizon, except maybe terrorism

Millennial Profiles – Ideology and "Special" Reality

World-wide

Some key findings [from] Deloitte's third annual Millennial Survey_of nearly 7,800 Millennials from 28 countries across Western Europe, North America, Latin America, BRICS, and Asia-Pacific about business, government, and innovation are:

• While most Millennials believe business is having a positive impact on society and increasing prosperity, they think business can do much more to address society's challenges in the areas of most concern: resource scarcity, climate change, and income inequality;
• 50 percent of Millennials surveyed want to work for a business with ethical practices;

- Millennials say government has the greatest potential to address society's biggest issues but are overwhelmingly failing to do so;
- Millennials believe the biggest barrier to innovation is management's attitude;
- Millennials believe the success of a business should be measured in terms of more than just its financial performance, with a focus on improving society among the most important things it should seek to achieve;
- Millennials are also charitable and keen to participate in "public life": donate to charities, actively volunteer, and be a member of a community organization.

In America

The Pew Center's massive new report on the state of affairs for the Millennial generation is full of contradictions about them. For example:

- Economic conditions for Millennials are atrocious, with high unemployment, yet they are the most optimistic of any generation;
- Millennials are the most technologically connected generation in history, yet also the least trusting of generations;
- The Millennial generation have the most number of single parents, yet has the most negative attitude toward single parents;
- The Millennial generation is the most educated generation in history and the deepest in debt for their education;
- While the economy has been the most prosperous in history, the Millennial generation will not likely live a better standard of living than their parents;
- While Millennials are more liberal than other generations on gay marriage, marijuana use, and immigration, they are not liberal on abortion and gun control;
- Millennials want universal health care but oppose Obamacare;
- Millennials say they care about the environment, but don't consider themselves environmentalists;

- Millennials have few attachments to traditional political and religious institutions.[43]

Boomerang Kids

In a well-documented trend, the number of young Americans living with their parents has grown over the last 15 years. Some have returned home after striking out on their own, earning the nickname "the boomerang generation," while others never left at all. One consequence of this is that home ownership among the young has fallen considerably.

Though the trend is clear, the question remains: What's driving it? Are poor job prospects causing the young to live with parents until a decent employment opportunity comes along? Has increased tuition and high debt levels from student loans forced students to stay at home while attending college, or return home to live less expensively while they pay off those debts? Are housing and rent too costly for them to live on their own, more so than for previous generations?

A new Federal Reserve Bank of New York staff report suggests the most important factor is the rising student debt of college graduates. This appears to be driving young people home and keeping them there. ...

In addition, the results demonstrate that local economic growth is a mixed blessing when it comes to building youth independence: Improvement in youth employment conditions enables young people to move away from their parents, but rising local house prices are estimated to have forced many young people to move back home. These two effects partially offset each other.[44]

---

[43] Retrieved from: https://www.psychologytoday.com/blog/wired-success/201403/how-the-millennial-generation-will-change-the-workplace

[44] Retrieved from: http://www.cbsnews.com/news/what-is-causing-the-boomerang-generation/

The disconnect between what America has "told" their children about what life is and will be, and with what America is and will be – _may cause deep mental unrest and disappointment!_

Millennials: Fight, Flight or Freeze Response to Disappointment

Freeze response

The fight or flight response (in its original form) is about survival. It's about hope. We activate it when we believe there's a chance we can outrun or outfight our attackers. The freeze response however, gets activated when's there's no hope.

In some respects, this response (whatever you call it) could be seen as an energy conservation device. It allowed our prehistoric ancestors to go through their day, using a modest amount of energy for mundane tasks while keeping a massive amount of energy, always on reserve, in case of emergency. If, while engaged in completing these mundane tasks, a predator were to jump out of the bushes, our ancestors would be able to – in a split second – dramatically increase their physical resources and instantly fight harder or run faster than they EVER had in their whole lives.

This response was very adaptive because it allowed our ancestors to change gears literally in the span of a single heartbeat. We can still do this today and call up this tremendous strength (the story about the woman who lifted a car off her son is NOT an urban legend) any time we need to and more importantly, turn it off when the danger passes....

For human beings, the freeze response can occur when we're terrified and feel like there is no chance for our survival or no chance for escape. It happens in car accidents, to rape victims and to people who are robbed at gunpoint. Sometimes they pass out, freeze or mentally remove themselves from their bodies, and don't feel the pain of the attack, and sometimes have no (explicit) memory of it afterwards.

68

That's why the fight or flight response is now called the fight, flight or freeze response. Because sometimes, when the odds are overwhelming we neither fight nor flee but simply freeze. And knowing this has special meaning in the treatment of trauma patients who, as survivors of a freeze event, experience flashbacks and other (implicit) memory fragments that can continue to haunt them for years afterwards.[45]

So Millennials may just be overwhelmed at the disparity between the world they were led to believe exists, and the one that DOES exist. Freeze.

<u>Flight Response</u>

It is unlikely the current generation will flee. There is nowhere to go!

<u>Fight Response</u>

-Deprivation-

In social comparison, **relative deprivation** is the experience of being deprived of something to which one believes oneself to be entitled. It refers to the discontent people feel when they compare their positions to others and realize that they have less of what they believe themselves to be entitled than those around them...

Social scientists, particularly political scientists and sociologists, have cited 'relative deprivation' (especially temporal relative deprivation) as a potential cause of social movements and deviance, leading in extreme situations to political violence such as rioting, terrorism, civil wars and other instances of social deviance such as crime. For example, some scholars of social movements explain their rise by citing grievances of people who feel deprived of what they perceive as

---

[45] Retrieved from: http://www.stressstop.com/stress-tips/articles/fight-flight-or-freeze-response-to-stress.php

values to which they are entitled. Similarly, individuals engage in deviant behaviors when their means do not match their goals.[46]

Responses to Means-Goals Conflict

-Acting Out-

To express a compulsive, hostile overt behavior through overt expression and damaging one's external environment.

-Acting In-

To express a compulsive, hostile overt behavior through repression and damaging one's internal environment. One's physical and/or mental health.

Examples of Frustrated Expectations, and the Consequences

Theater Mass Shooting

On July 20, 2012, a mass shooting occurred inside of a Century 16 movie theater in Aurora, Colorado, during a midnight screening of the film *The Dark Knight Rises*. A gunman, dressed in tactical clothing, set off tear gas grenades and shot into the audience with multiple firearms. Twelve people were killed and seventy others were injured, the largest number of casualties in a shooting in the United States. The sole assailant, James Eagan Holmes, was arrested in his car parked outside the cinema minutes later. It was the deadliest shooting in Colorado since the Columbine High School massacre in 1999. Prior to the shooting, Holmes rigged his apartment with homemade explosives, which were defused by a bomb squad one day after the shooting....

---

[46] Retrieved from: http://psychology.wikia.com/wiki/Relative_deprivation

70

Holmes confessed to the shooting but pleaded not guilty by reason of insanity. Arapahoe County prosecutors sought the death penalty for Holmes. The trial began on April 27, 2015. He was convicted of twenty-four counts of first-degree murder, 140 counts of attempted first-degree murder, and one count of possessing explosives on July 16, 2015. On August 7, 2015, he was sentenced to life in prison without the possibility of parole... -- Wikipedia

Holmes' expectations:

James Holmes, the Aurora shooter, was apparently prowling for a one-night stand in the days leading up to the "Dark Knight Massacre," only to be rejected three times.

It was previously reported and later confirmed that James Holmes was an active member on *Adult FriendFinder*, a website used to arrange one-night stands, group sex, etc. The profile was removed by site administrators. He had apparently been reaching out to multiple women in the weeks leading up to the attack, only to be turned down by each and every one of them, reports *TMZ*....

Though Holmes adopted a seemingly harmless approach on a website designed for hook-ups, his profile suggested that he was down for all sorts of lewd acts, that he was primarily looking for a "casual sex" arrangement, that he was open to the possibility of a threesome with a male/female couple, and that he showed interest in attending group sex parties....

Holmes was also rejected by a shooting range, according to *Politico*. He applied to join the Lead Valley Range in Byers on June 25. The owner called the number listed on the application to follow-up and invite Holmes to a mandatory orientation, but the call went to voice-mail. After hearing a "bizarre – guttural, freakish at best," message, he decided to decline membership to Holmes.[47]

And

I have been reading a lot about the James Holmes "Dark Knight" massacre lately. Many of my colleagues here on PsychologyToday.com have given their own theories on the matter. I'd like to add my own—which is a little bit different...

Truth be told, I don't believe Holmes is as unique or deviant as it would be comfortable to think. This type of behavior is on the rise. So, I think we need to look beyond the individual for the cause. We need to look past the symbols of Batman and Joker in this particular case. We need to look beyond "pathologizing" the person, to understanding the social and systemic factors that are creating such behavior....

It is clear that Holmes is angry and violent. Many have suggested that it was due to his failing in school. Perhaps latent narcissism or mental illness. But, beyond labeling him a "loner", few have looked at Holmes' social life....

So, James Holmes was rejected by women... How does that lead to killing? To answer that question, we need to take a step back.

Initially, James Holmes did everything right that society told him to do. He was a "good guy". He was smart, ambitious, motivated. He had a good life ahead of him. In years past, that would have made him very desirable to women. In today's world, however, it didn't get him very far... Today, it made him a loner and a nerd, with no social skills and no dating prospects.

---

[47] Retrieved from: http://www.inquisitr.com/283225/james-holmes-was-rejected-by-three-women-prior-to-aurora-shooting/

Why then turn from a nerd to a killer? That is, unfortunately, very simple. More women love killers than nerds. Being a killer today is more socially and sexually rewarding than being a "good guy". Countless women write love letters and beg for conjugal visits to death row inmates…. Even Holmes himself has already begun collecting adoring female fans on Twitter who think he is "hot", "sexy", and "cute….[48]

Workplace Shooting

A shooting incident occurred at a firm in Minneapolis, Minnesota, on the afternoon of Thursday, September 27, 2012. The attack took place inside Accent Signage Systems, where a former employee walked into the firm's building and fired a Glock 19 9mm pistol. By the end of the day, five people were dead, including the gunman who committed suicide, and four others were injured, three of them critically. One of those critically injured died the following day, and another man succumbed to his wounds on October 10. It was the deadliest workplace shooting in Minnesota's history.

Engeldinger's disappointment:

The shooting took place at Accent Signage Systems, a sign-making business located in the Bryn Mawr neighborhood of Minneapolis, which is bisected by Interstate 394. Andrew John Engeldinger, an employee of the firm, was called over to the office of operations director John Souter. Before going to the executive offices, Engeldinger first went to his car, apparently to retrieve a Glock 19 9mm handgun. When he was informed by Souter that he was losing his job, Engeldinger responded with "Oh, really?" and took out the handgun from his holster. A struggle over the handgun ensued between Engeldinger, Souter, and top manager Rami Cooks; gunshots severely wounded Souter and fatally wounded Cooks. Engeldinger then left

[48] Retrieved from: https://www.psychologytoday.com/blog/the-attraction-doctor/201208/james-holmes-mental-illness-or-social-frustration

Souter's office, shooting and killing company founder Reuven Rahamim, who was stepping out of his office, which was next to Souter's. He then left the executive offices and entered a sign-display area, killing Jacob Beneke, an employee from Maple Grove. Engeldinger then moved on to the loading dock area, where he shot and killed a second employee, Ronald Edberg of Brooklyn Center. He also killed Keith Basinski, a UPS driver who was on a delivery, as he was seated in his truck. Engeldinger then entered the production floor and continued firing, fatally wounding production manager Eric Rivers and grazing another employee. – Wikipedia

Traditional Stress Safety Valve Jammed

The original immigrants to America from Europe we brave rebels who got tired of being marginalized, screwed over by a rich minority, broken justice system, lack or opportunity to progress, etc.

They literally risked their lives to get to the east coast of America. And a fresh start.

The next wave of disappointed people were those who pushed west, all the way to California eventually.

Now there is no "new frontier" for disappointed Americans to go, except maybe northern Canada.

The social pressure due to dissidents is building!

The Next Big Looming Disappointment – Hunger

Hungry humans are animalized rather than civilized by hunger.

The US 2016 poverty guidelines for Alaska, for example, are:

Persons in family/household	Poverty guideline
1	$14,840
2	20,020
3	25,200
4	30,380
5	35,560
6	40,740
7	45,920
8	51,120

In 2012 the percentage of seniors living in poverty was 14% while 18% of children were.[49]

In some States a large percentage of citizens are taking food stamps, as high as 50%.

Schools now routinely provide breakfast and lunch, to prevent stunted brain development. This includes summer programs.

SCORE	ISSUE
-1	Adequate food (barring Nature's interventions)
-1	Repression of animal savagery
-2	Fear from harm from outside the community
-2	Fear from harm from inside the community
-1	Acceptance of authority and class structure
-1	Stable government
-2	Crime rate
-2	Fair justice system
-1	Adequate control of Nature & Human behavior

---

[49] US Census Bureau, September 2013.

CHAPTER 7: THE UNITED STATES IS A TRAIN WRECK IN SLOW MOTION!

Model: The Rise and Fall of Past Civilizations

Civilizations usually begin at the hunter-gatherer/agricultural level. They rise to a peak level. Then most sink into a "dark age". Some sink further into continual chaos, subject to invasion, and easily overtaken by warfare.

Adapted from[50]:

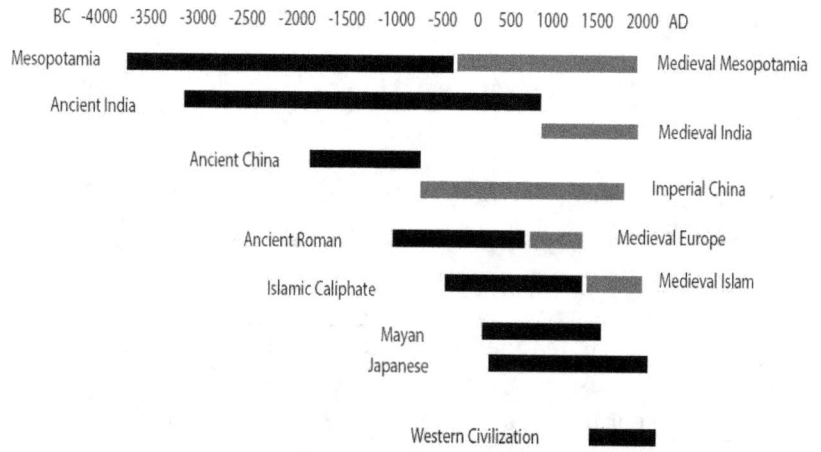

Model: The Rise and Fall of Contemporary Civilizations

A democracy cannot exist as a permanent form of government. It can only exist until the voters discover that they can vote themselves largess of the public treasury. From that time on the majority always votes for the candidates promising the most benefits from the public treasury, with the results that a

---

[50] http://www.mikeanderson.biz/2010/02/great-civilizations-of-antiquity.html

democracy always collapses over loose fiscal policy, always followed by a dictatorship...

The average age of the world's greatest civilizations has been two hundred years. These nations have progressed through this sequence: from bondage to spiritual faith; from spiritual faith to great courage; from great courage to liberty; from liberty to abundance; from abundance to selfishness; from selfishness to complacency; from complacency to apathy; from apathy to dependence; from dependency back again to bondage. – Sir Alex Fraser Tyler (1742-1813) Scottish jurist and historian.

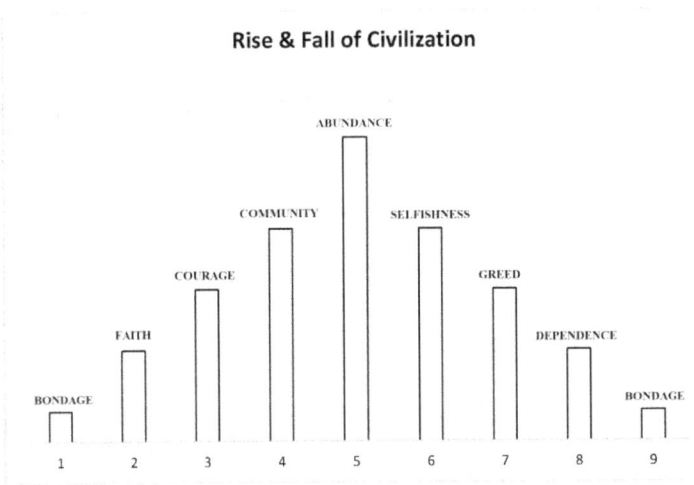

Rise & Fall of Civilization

By this criterion, the United States is well over the hill.

Markers of a Civilization

Although it is freely given that "measures of civilization stability" could be defined in many ways, let's follow[51]:

<u>Elements that distinguish civilizations that survived</u>

    A. Natural barriers against invaders

    B. Reliable agriculture, predictable harvests, fertile, and abundant soil

    C. Self-sufficiency, less need for imports

    D. Divine or semi-divine kingship.

By These Criteria, the United States Is <u>Not</u> Destined To Survive As a Civilization

<u>Natural Barriers to Invaders</u>

In the early days of the United States, the oceans (and Great Britain's naval dominance) protected the new nation.

These days, that protection is gone. There are airplanes, submarines, intercontinental missiles, and terrorist cells.

<u>Reliable Agriculture, Predictable Harvests</u>

Due to coast-coast El Nino/La Nina patterns, climate change, and over- and under-abundance of water, the unpredictable threatens reliable food production.

Due to Global Warming, freeze patterns are no longer predictable.

---

[51] Retrieved from: http://faculty.citadel.edu/frank.karpiel/class04riseandfall.pdf

Self-sufficiency, Less Need for Imports

Due to job outsourcing/off shoring, moving manufacturing facilities off shore, and the interdependence of global financial systems, the United States (as mentioned before) is HIGHLY/OVERLY dependent upon imports and the swings with fortunes of <u>other</u> countries.

Divine or Semi-divine Kingship

"Trust" in United States institutional government is at an all-time low, except for the Military.

In a report from the Gallup Polling Company reporting the last week of March, 2016[52], Americans said that the percentage of them "mostly, or almost always" trusted was:

Military	39%
Supreme Court	30%
Executive	29%
Police	25%
Congress	7%

Note: You might recall that during the "Arab Spring" revolutions, the Military were the instrument of regime and constitutional form change. America is poised at this same point?

Other Holes in the United States "Civilized" Facade

I will add three additional serious weaknesses in the United States' well-being.

---

[52] Retrieved from: http://www.washingtonexaminer.com/dangerous-precedent-americans-have-greater-faith-in-police-military-than-three-branches-of-u.s.-government/article/2550353

*Leisure Time and Entertainment Addiction

Fifty-plus years ago, in the old model, I remember living in some pretty dumpy houses. Of course, at that age I didn't know the difference. I do remember almost all of my Christmas and Birthday gifts being school clothes.

There were a couple major illnesses my parents went through, and things got really tight financially.

In my teens, my Mother got Cancer, and so as to not have to think about the axe hanging over her head, went to work. I was left alone most afternoons, but I had LOTS of High School homework, the custom of those times. And household chores I inherited from my working mother.

My parents had both made the jump from blue collar to white collar work, and were fighting the snarky world of the white collar environment. In the blue collar world, when someone snipes at and demeans you, they get a bloody nose. In white collar work, one has to be more "civilized". For my parents, that meant a huge burden of fatigue and mental anguish from stuffed down insults, when they were home. We began to live better (house, clothes, car), but much worse in terms of stress.

(This class-based stress ultimately led to my parent's early demise.)

The end of the week, Sunday Night, all our household, yard and my homework were done. We took one hour to watch "Adventures in Paradise" on TV before going to bed and waking up to another grueling week ahead.

Today's model: adults and children (in the dwindling Middle Class) have a great deal of leisure time, relative wealth, and are addicted to entertainment: TV, games, and gadgets (like smart phones, which now host all of these).

Instead of spending their leisure time understanding themselves, improving their mental skills, or contributing to their less fortunate neighbors, they are glued to their entertainment centers, from room size to palm size.

In previous ages, the VERY few people with leisure time engaged in Natural Philosophy, invention, and altruism – all of which bootstrapped their societies.

The United States is in the "me" generation, not the "we" generation. There are no common goals/national programs/enemies, just me-time.

Of course, as mentioned above, there ARE national (if not World) serious problems now, and ahead in time. But there are few people willing to assess, plan in an organized way, nor act against any of these "enemies" to survival of the nation. The "government" is trying to hold onto slipping personal control and fortunes. No one is "watching the store!"

*Stagnation of Innovation

In the 2013 article in *Paravaratin*,

> The top 50 inventions over time were assessed In the November 2013 issues of the Atlantic, James Fellows interviews a panel of historians, scientists and technologist from MIT to the Silicon Valley Powerhouse Kleiner Perkins Caufield & Byers on what are the top 50 breakthrough inventions since the wheel....[53]:

---

[53] http://blog.stephenwolfram.com/2011/08/advance-of-the-data-civilization-a-timeline/

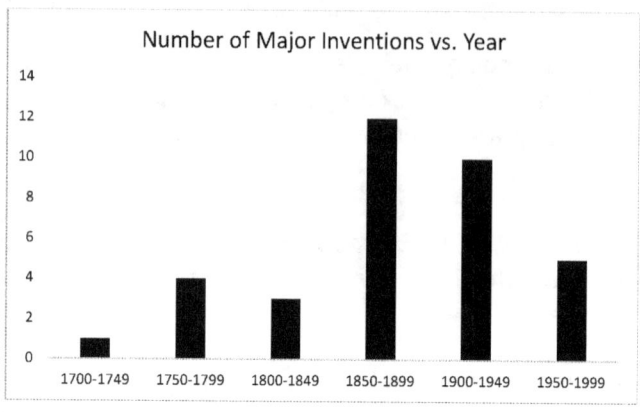

A quick glance at the chart above [adapted from the above article] shows a rapid pace of innovation during 1850-1899 (12 inventions) and 1900-1949 (10 inventions). Indeed, someone living through the period would have seen everything from the invention of the automobile and airplanes to rocketry and nuclear fission. Breakthroughs like those since the 1950s have been far and few between.

As noted by James Fellow, there is a view that perhaps this was a special period in human history – the apex of many decades of low-hanging fruit – that cannot be repeated again….

Stagnation in innovation means that actual system-shocking innovation will be increasingly rare and will requirement momental [sic] investments….

The very common American assumption that one's life will be substantially better than their parents *as a default* will fade as unbounded optimism and hope in technology fades. Governments will have to be more effective than ever to deliver on goods and services, as "faith in the markets" cannot be depended on to give greater opportunities (in innovation, jobs, living standards) by itself.[54]

*Warfare for the Sole Purpose of Homeland Control, the Need to Bully, and for Profiteering

Since the Viet Nam War, the United States has been engaging in "policing actions", overtly purported to be for protection of "innocents" from "oppression".

There has always been a more pessimistic and sinister interpretation of these actions:

-War as a Choice-

Regarding oil resources, for decades the oil resource was held by Middle Eastern countries. In fact, oil is their only natural resource – discounting sand.

Fifty years ago, I remember a visiting British couple. In casual conversation over rather they could afford a music recording, they shared that when home in Britain, and they had to save a whole month to afford the gasoline for a weekend car trip.

They were paying the "price" of the gasoline. In dollars (pounds), not in lives. Inconvenience was tolerated.

In the United States, we can play the "pride" card, bully the Middle East with endless wars and forced regime changes, drive down the gasoline prices, and pay with a vast-multiple number or war-dollars (compared to gas dollars), and with lives!

Which is more costly, inconvenience or lives?

---

[54] Retrieved from: http://parivartin.com/2013/10/the-invention-stagnation-in-a-single-chart/

-Controlling a Restless Homeland Population-

Quoting,

"I don't want a nation of thinkers. I want a nation of workers."
John D. Rockefeller.

The Rockefeller's founded the National Education Association.

WHISTLEBLOWER
September 1, 2001

Dumbed Down

**The Deliberate Destruction of the
American Education System**

** *Reproduction of what was within quote.*

Perhaps you may now realize that through Random House, Webster and Oxford Press omissions, you are a victim of information control. Mind control is sometimes loosely defined as information control. This being one of many accepted ways to define the term should immediately raise questions of distrust towards your information sources. Since what we think is based on what we learn, manipulation of a mind, or a nation of minds, can be accomplished through control of information. With thought control being a result of information control, many avid researchers of mind sciences simply label it "soft" mind control....

The man of the household must be house-broken to ensure that junior will grow up with the right social training and attitudes. The advertising media, etc., are engaged to see to it that father-to-be is pussy-whipped before or by the time he is married. He is taught that he either conforms to the social notch out for him or his sex life will be hobbled and his tender companionship will be zero. He is made to see that women demand security more than logical, principled, or honorable behavior. By the time his son must go to war, father (with jelly for a back bone) will slam a gun into junior's hand before father will risk the censure of his peers, or make a hypocrite of himself by crossing the investment he has in his own personal opinion or self-esteem. Junior will go to war or father will be embarrassed. So junior will go to war, the true purpose of the war notwithstanding....[55]

The United States government agencies during war-time instigated several mind-control research programs:

> **MKULTRA** focused on drugs, specifically LSD since the CIA had a phobia about LSD ending up in the hands of the Russians. The CIA wanted to use LSD as a weapon. The Russians and the Cold War were used as a national security excuse for most of the CIA's actions. The CIA studied hundreds of other drugs besides LSD, as well as experimenting with: "radiation, electroshock, psychology, sociology, anthropology, psychiatry, harassment substances and paramilitary devices and materials." It appears that the scientists enjoyed trying these drugs on themselves, but they also used many hospital patients, volunteers (mostly students), inmates who were usually paid for their participation with more drugs, and eventually anyone the CIA could get, without their consent, of course. The CIA "scientists" even reduced themselves to misting and spraying unwitting American citizens as they walked down busy city streets. Later they would study how they could manipulate genes, and develop compounds that could simulate heart attack and stroke....

> **Mockingbird** - This unlikely land of enchantment is the creation of MOCKINGBIRD. It was conceived in the late 1940s,

---

[55] http://www.theforbiddenknowledge.com/hardtruth/mind_control_index.htm

the most frigid period of the cold war, when the CIA began a systematic infiltration of the corporate media, a process that often included direct takeover of major news outlets. In this period, the American intelligence services competed with communist activists abroad to influence European labor unions. With or without the cooperation of local governments, Frank Wisner, an undercover State Department official assigned to the Foreign Service, rounded up students abroad to enter the cold war underground of covert operations on behalf of his Office of Policy Coordination. Philip Graham, a graduate of the Army Intelligence School in Harrisburg, PA, then publisher of the Washington Post., was taken under Wisner's wing to direct the program code-named Operation MOCKINGBIRD

Operation MOCKINGBIRD — The CIA begins recruiting American news organizations and journalists to become spies and disseminators of propaganda. The effort is headed by Frank Wisner, Allan Dulles, Richard Helms and Philip Graham. Graham is publisher of The Washington Post, which becomes a major CIA player. Eventually, the CIA's media assets will include ABC, NBC, CBS, Time, Newsweek, Associated Press, United Press International, Reuters, Hearst Newspapers, Scripps-Howard, Copley News Service and more. By the CIA's own admission, at least 25 organizations and 400 journalists will become CIA assets....[56]

Anecdotally, I am a Physicist. After the Cold War with the Soviet Union, I met several faculty members who were Russian immigrants. We all agreed that we, Scientists, were lied to by Generals as to the actual threat from the other side so that we would cooperate in whatever research our governments asked of us out of patriotism.

There was also a control/prestige/profiteering conspiracy by Generals on both side of the Cold War.

---

[56] Ibid.

-Profiteering-

In World War II:

Lee's best-known excess came in September, at the height of the supply crisis. Eisenhower had frequently expressed his view that no major headquarters should be located in or near the temptations of a large city, and had specifically reserved the hotels in Paris for the use of combat troops on leave. Lee nevertheless, and without Eisenhower's knowledge, moved his headquarters to Paris. His people requisitioned all the hotels previously occupied by the Germans, and took over schools and other large buildings. More than 8,000 officers and 21,000 men in SOS descended on the city in less than a week, with tens of thousands more to follow. Parisians began to mutter that the U.S. Army demands were in excess of those made by the Germans.

The GIs and their generals were furious. They stated the obvious at the height of the supply crisis, Lee had spent his precious time organizing the move, then used up precious gasoline, all so that he and his entourage could enjoy the hotels of Paris. It got worse. With 29,000 SOS troops in Paris, the great majority of them involved in some way in the flow of supplies from the beaches and ports to the front, and taking into account what Paris had to sell, from wine and girls to jewels and perfumes, a black market on a grand scale sprang up.

Eisenhower was enraged. He sent a firm order to Lee to stop the entry into Paris of every individual not absolutely essential and to move out of the city every man who was not. He said essential duties "will not include provision of additional facilities, services and recreation for SOS or its Headquarters." He told Lee that he would like to order him out of the city altogether, but could not afford to waste more gasoline in moving SOS again. He said Lee had made an "extremely unwise" decision and told him to correct the situation as soon as possible.

Of course Lee and his headquarters stayed in Paris. And of course there was solid reason for so doing. And of course the combat veterans who got three-day passes into Paris could never get a hotel room, and had to sleep in a barracks-like Red Cross shelter, on cots. The rear-echelon SOS got the beds and private rooms. And their numbers grew rather than shrank. By March 1945, there were 160,000 SOS troops in the Department of the Seine.

The supply troops also got the girls, because they had the money, thanks to the black market. It flourished everywhere. Thousands of gallons of gasoline, tons of food and clothing, millions of cigarettes, were being siphoned off each day. The gasoline pipeline running from the beaches to Chartres was tapped so many times only a trickle came out at the far end.

Most of this was petty thievery. It was done at the expense of the front-line troops. As one example, the most popular brand of cigarettes was Lucky Strike, followed by Camel. In Paris, the SOS troops and their dates smoked Lucky Strikes and Camels; in the foxholes, the men got Pall Malls, Raleighs, or, worse, British cigarettes.

But a large part of the black market was run by organized crime. Here is a story told to me by a former lieutenant who worked as a criminal investigator for the SHAEF adjutant general's office. There was a colonel from the National Guard, born in Sicily, who was in Transport Command. His administrative job gave him the use of a C-47. On every clear day he flew, with a co-pilot, from London to Paris and back. He took in cartons of cigarettes and brought back jewels and perfumes. His trade flourished but there were a lot of payoffs to make, too many people involved. By mid-December, SHAEF's criminal investigators were ready to arrest him, but he got a tip and fled in his C47, with a co-pilot and a box stuffed with jewelry.

"Over the Channel," the lieutenant told me, "he shot the copilot, then smashed his face beyond recognition. He was a hell of a pilot; he landed on the edge of the water at an extremely low tide near Utah Beach. The plane with the co-pilot's body wasn't found until the next day's low tide -- and the major had left his dog tags on the dead man. We learned later that a French farm couple had watched an American pilot as he stole a donkey and cart, loaded a box onto the cart, slipped into peasant's clothing, and was last seen headed toward Sicily."[57]

-Oil as the Motive-

Finally, there is strong evidence to back up a popular conspiracy theory — oil is often the motivating reason that one country interferes in another country's war. Likewise, the researchers say, third party states may decide not to step into ongoing intrastate conflicts if there is no crude incentive. For example, a lack of oil is "said to be behind the absence of intervention in Syria now and in Rwanda in 1994", say two of the authors of a new *Journal of Conflict Resolution* paper.

Civil wars have made up more than 90 percent of all armed conflicts since World War II and, during that period, countries that need oil have found reasons to militarily intervene in countries with a good supply of it, according to the study. In "Oil above Water — Economic Interdependence and Third-party Intervention" the researchers explain how they modelled the decision-making process used by third-party countries to determine whether to interfere in civil wars and examined their economic motives.

In their research, the UK team — Petros Sekeris of University of Portsmouth, Vincenzo Bove from the University of Warwick and Kristian Skrede Gleditsch of the University of Essex — looked at 69 countries that experienced civil conflicts between 1945 and 1999. They found that about two-thirds of these wars

[57] Retrieved from: http://www.worldwar2history.info/Army/profiteers.html

saw intervention by another country or outside organization and that the most common reason for this intervention, "over and above historical, geographical or ethnic ties", was oil.

"We wanted to go beyond conspiracy theories and conduct a careful, nuanced analysis to see whether oil acts as an economic incentive in the decision on whether to intervene in an internal war in another country," explained Sekeris.

Military intervention is expensive and risky. No country joins another country's civil war without balancing the cost against their own strategic interests and what possible benefits there are.

The results show that outsiders are much more motivated to join a fight if they have a vested financial interest.

Indeed, among their findings the team determined that the more oil a country has, the more likely it is that a third party will intervene in their civil war. And on the flipside, the more oil a country imports, the greater the likelihood it will intervene in an oil-producing country's civil war.

Among the examples highlighted are the United States' involvement in Angola's civil war from 1975 to the end of the Cold War and in Guatemala, Indonesia and the Philippines. The authors also point to US support of conservative autocratic states in oil-rich regions. Also cited were the UK's involvement in Nigeria's 1967-70 civil war, in contrast to the non-intervention in civil wars in other former colonies with no oil reserves (Sierra Leone and Rhodesia, later Zimbabwe); and the former Soviet Union's involvement in Indonesia (1958), Nigeria (1967-68) and Iraq (1973).

The 'thirst for oil' is often put forward as a near self-evident explanation behind the intervention in Libya and the absence of intervention in Syria. Many claims are often simplistic but, after a rigorous and systematic analysis, we found that the role of economic incentives emerges as a key factor in intervention," Vincenzo Bove said.

The team found that a third party country was more likely to intervene if:

> They were a major power;
> The rebels were strong and well-armed;
> There were close ethnic ties between the two countries; and/or
> The civil war took place during the Cold War, a period of global competition between superpowers.

Then, at the other end of the spectrum, there are the oil-rich states that don't do much intervening at all — nations including the Gulf States, Mexico and Indonesia that have no history of military intervention in other countries' civil wars, despite having well equipped military forces.

Twenty-first century intervention: "Before the ISIS forces approached the oil-rich Kurdish north of Iraq, ISIS was barely mentioned in the news. But once ISIS got near oil fields, the siege of Kobani in Syria became a headline and the US sent drones to strike ISIS targets," Bove said.

The enduring record of geopolitical instability in oil producing regions and the likely increase in the global demand for oil means we'll see more of these interventions in future, Sekaris and Bove predict.

However, there will be some big changes in who is intervening where, they say. With shale gas, the US is becoming less energy dependent, while China's continued growth will see it needing energy imports more than ever.

These interventions should in turn lead to stronger economic ties. Research we carried out with Leandro Elia, published in the *Review of International Economics*, found strong empirical evidence that US troop deployment and military aid provokes an expansion in bilateral trade flows.[58]

Conclusion?

Remember what happens in the animal kingdom to the slothful and unwatchful? Is America slothful and blasé?

Or have we truly entered an age of existence without resistance, as we have portrayed to our children?

Or is the United States just completely in tatters, delusional, and rudderless?

---

[58] Retrieved from: http://theconversation.com/are-crude-conspiracies-right-research-shows-nations-really-do-go-to-war-over-oil-36846